YES MA'AM,
NO SIR

YES MA'AM, NO SIR

The *12*
Essential Steps for
Success in Life

COACH CARTER

**BUSINESS
PLUS**

NEW YORK   BOSTON

Business Plus
Hachette Book Group
237 Park Avenue
New York, NY 10017

www.HachetteBookGroup.com

Business Plus is an imprint of Grand Central Publishing.
The Business Plus name and logo are trademarks of
Hachette Book Group, Inc.

The publisher is not responsible for websites (or their content)
that are not owned by the publisher.

Printed in the United States of America

RRD-C

First Edition: February 2012
10 9 8 7 6 5 4 3 2 1

Library of Congress Cataloging-in-Publication Data

Carter, Ken (Kenneth Ray)
Yes ma'am, no sir : the 12 essential steps for success in life /
by Ken Carter.—1st ed.
p. cm.
ISBN 978-1-4555-0234-9
1. Carter, Ken (Kenneth Ray)   2. Conduct of life.   3. Values.   4. Success.
5. Success in business.   I. Title.
BJ1581.2.C2547   2012
158—dc23
2011021220

This book is dedicated to my parents,
the late A. J. Carter, Sr., and
my mother, Hettie Lee Carter.

Contents

Contents

Author's Note

I love to learn. It doesn't matter what subject we're talking about; if it's something I don't know, then I want to learn about it, and if it's something I already know about, then I want to learn more.

I have an insatiable curiosity about all forms of human behavior and about life in general. Everything in this world fills me with wonder. That's exactly what happened when I picked up a pen to write this book. I couldn't put it down because when I went to work on this book, this book went to work on me. I learned something from every sentence!

If you are in possession of this book, I consider you a part of my team, and as part of my team, it is crucial that you win.

So read this book. Pick it apart and take notes, because this is the playbook to success in your life.

YES MA'AM, NO SIR

Introduction

Long before I became "Coach Carter" of Hollywood recognition, portrayed in the blockbuster film by Samuel L. Jackson, I was Kennie Ray Carter, a boy who watched his parents tirelessly raise nine children on a farm in rural Mississippi.

As it turned out, it was the perfect backdrop to an inspired life that has become a touchstone of limitless possibilities and success.

I was too young to see that then. Instead, I wondered: Why do we seem to have less than others?

We weren't poor; we were broke. Being broke is just an economic condition. But being poor is a disabling frame of mind and a depressed condition of the human spirit. So we were never, ever depressed. We were just broke.

I tell people that my family was so broke that when we rode by the bank, we set off the alarm.

The reality, I came to understand, was that even though we were broke, we had more than most: more love and support and togetherness, and those elements sustained us and helped shape me into a man of honor, commitment, and achievement.

It was a long journey that started when I was a kid. Seeing my parents work hard to provide for us instilled a dogged work ethic in me that showed when I was just seven years old—and it still resides in me today.

At that young age I started my first business. I placed small, undeveloped cucumbers inside long-neck bottles and waited until they grew to where they could not come out. It made people wonder how I got the big cucumber through the narrow bottleneck.

I loaded up my unique novelties into my little red wagon, and with no shoes or shirt, I headed into town to set up shop.

I sold them for five dollars. If someone had a ten-dollar bill, I never gave him change. Instead, I sold him two. I just had no fear. And I ended up making more in a day than my mom and dad.

That was where my road to being a leader began. Years later, when our family moved across the country to Richmond, California, I carried that spirit of owner-ship and leadership with me.

The day we arrived in Richmond was March 19, 1972. I remember that day so well all these years later because so much happened. We were excited to move into a home with running water; in Mississippi, I had to pump water from a well.

Also, that was the day I met Mr. James Dunkley. He owned a Laundromat in Richmond, and that first day I saw him dump hundreds of quarters from the washers and dryers into a big bucket. Back in Mississippi, if you had a quarter, you had wealth. And here was this man with hundreds of them.

I was only twelve, but I could not resist asking Mr. Dunkley, "Are all those quarters yours?" He told me they were and that he emptied the machines twice a week.

Well, I was mesmerized. That made a real impression on me, but not as much as what Mr. Dunkley said to me that day:

"You can make a life for yourself working for others. You can create a lifestyle if you work for yourself."

Powerful. That stuck with me. And it is one of the principles I still carry with me today.

In one sense, Mr. Dunkley meant that it was important to have leadership over your life, to take command of it. Too often, I have found that most people do not know how to do that. They get set into a mundane routine and exist instead of creating a winning lifestyle for themselves.

I play to win—and I'm not just talking about basketball. My name and some of my story are familiar because of the motion picture that depicted an integral part of my life.

But what I accomplished with the young men on the Richmond High School basketball team was far more than about the results of the games. Those results were extremely important; you play the game to win, and we were so adamant about it that I never even kept any second-place trophy we received.

But the bigger and more important part of that

experience was the teaching of leadership and discipline and self-pride and work ethic. Those are the character traits that had to be built up as we went on the basketball journey.

They called me "Coach Carter," but I called myself a teacher. A coach designs plays and sets up specific things for a player to do on the court. A teacher explains why you do certain things to get the desired results.

My players learned about the game and the fundamentals and how to attack an opponent based on knowing their strengths and weaknesses and understanding basketball. That's not coaching; that's teaching.

When I first got there, we had no nets on the goals, no socks, no towels, which didn't matter because the showers didn't work. But the only thing that bothered me was that our boys looked like losers—and they acted like losers.

So I told them, "All that changes. Today. Winning in here is the same as winning out there, in life."

If you take a basketball and hold it over your head and drop it, every time it bounces, it loses fifty percent of its momentum. That's the way a basketball career is. Every year someone comes behind you a little bit stronger, a little bit faster, a little hungrier.

Every shot you take, you're getting closer to the end of your career. But hopefully you're getting a little bit smarter. You want to talk numbers? Only one in every five hundred thousand people even gets an opportunity to play any type of professional sports.

So it's okay to put all your eggs in one basket if it's the

family business and you have control of it—but not in becoming a professional player.

And that's how we went about our business. I have owned a sporting goods store, a T-shirt printing company, and four barbershops. They were all run professionally, as a business should be run. And I ran my basketball teams as a business, too.

The business was winning and making sure those kids were prepared to win in life. That mind-set developed for me unusually early in life. For most, it comes much later, if at all. And that's where this book comes in.

Through sharing my life experiences and the philosophies I developed through them, I will impart invaluable nuggets to maximize the winner in you so you, too, can gain or reinforce leadership over your life.

This will be an authentic journey that brings home the importance of taking ownership of your life to live a valued life of achievement, respect, and gratification.

Chapter One

Why Leadership Matters

It was a surreal feeling to see part of my life played out on celluloid in the 2005 motion picture *Coach Carter.* The feelings from those years came rushing back, like water over a breached levee. With every scene, a sense of pride and accomplishment covered my body.

The apex of the movie, in particular, brought me right back to the emotions of that time and place: I locked out my Richmond High basketball team from the gymnasium, causing much upheaval. We just so happened to be the top-ranked team in 1999 in California at the time, making my decision all the more dramatic.

The reason I went to such an extreme measure? Not all the players were maintaining a 2.3 grade point average.

As a former athlete, I knew how much they lived for game day. It was everything. But I locked them out because, as their leader, I had to make them understand that what they did in the classroom was more important than on the basketball court.

I had given them a contract that called for them to maintain a 2.3 GPA, to attend all their classes, to sit in the front of the classroom, and to wear a white shirt and tie to school on every game day, among other edicts. They signed it, meaning they were bound by it.

My academic challenge was significant in this way: To get into college with a 2.0 GPA, the students would have been required to score 850 on the SAT. With a 2.3, the requirement on the SAT was about one hundred points less. And because scoring more on the SAT is harder than raising your GPA in school, it made sense to me to make that a contractual goal for the players.

But some of the players basked too brightly in our 13–0 record, and their grades dropped. When I received the progress reports, I was devastated. The team's play had galvanized the school and the community. But I was also determined to use it as a teaching moment. So I locked the gym and canceled practices and games.

I was really tested then because the parents and even some of the faculty and administration at Richmond High were livid and did not agree with my actions. All of the kids had made the 2.0 GPA required by the district to be eligible to play. But not all of them had met the standards of the contract.

Some argued that the players who'd maintained at least a 2.3 average should have been allowed to play.

But that worked against everything I was instilling in the players about being part of a team: We win together and we lose together.

Although my actions in pursuing the "lockout" stirred great controversy and initiated a national media firestorm, it seemed to be a simple matter to me.

My players had given me their word, and now some of them had broken it. And when I became their basketball coach, I had given the players *my* word that I would uphold the standards of behavior and classroom performance that I had established for membership on the basketball team. The idea of controversy had never occurred to me. I was simply doing what my father and mother had taught me to do: I was living up to my word, and I expected my players to do the same.

But my actions did attract controversy. Lots of it. Sadly, it was rare that an adult would go to extremes to teach young men the value of upholding their word. That is a sad, but true, fact. Because it was pretty much unheard of that a coach would lock out his players, my exploits were written about in newspapers and magazines and discussed on television talk shows across America.

I received thousands of letters of congratulations from parents, young people, teachers, and civic leaders everywhere who believed in my stance, and I was on national news shows talking about my position.

All that attention came down on me, but everything was about the young men. Even though we had won thirteen games in a row to start the season, I had to teach them the lesson of accountability. And I knew that lesson hit home when the school board voted, 4–2, to end the lockout and reopen the gym.

I was prepared to quit my position as coach. I was that committed to my beliefs. But when I got to the gym, the players—these young men who love to play the game—decided they would forfeit games as they worked to pull up their grades. I knew for sure how special they were—and that they were growing as young men.

We forfeited four games before the grades were raised to the standard. California Governor Gray Davis attended our first game after the lockout, and I was later named Educator of the Year by Harvard University. Still, I never lost sight of who the real stars were: my players, who were growing into leaders from the leadership they experienced with me.

That was the most satisfying element of our journey. To see their growth was amazingly rewarding. I said many times: I went to work at Richmond High, and Richmond High worked on me from 1997 to 2003. We grew together.

I remember being at odds with the producers of *Coach Carter* for months during filming. They kept saying, "Coach, you've got to win the last game [in the movie]." I was like, "No. If you lose in the playoffs, that's the end. We wanted a storybook ending, but the reality was that we lost in the playoffs. And I wanted the movie to ring true. Plus, sometimes there is a bigger lesson in losing than winning.

They were saying, "How do we make this a winning movie? How do people leave the theater feeling good if you don't win the last game?" I said, "Sir, look at what my boys have done off the court, in the classroom."

And that was it.

That was bigger than anything else. That drove home the essence of leadership and the true purpose of our experience. Every player who played for me graduated. Every one. You come into a situation like I did, and you have to know it was bigger than basketball.

Sure, we wanted to win and we won a lot. But as the coach of the team, I had to be a leader. I had led in other areas of my life, and I had led myself. But this responsibility was enormous.

Richmond High was my school, in my community. I could see myself in those boys. It was important to establish that I cared, which was why I had them all sign the contract.

A significant part of the job was psychological. The boys were somewhat defeated in how they looked at life. They were unaware of the potential they possessed because few people let them know there was more out there for them.

This is why leadership matters—because someone needs to be led.

The contract they signed gave them parameters to work within, and I knew if they honored it, their self-esteem would be bolstered. I let it be known that it was a privilege to be a part of the team, to wear the uniform, to have the access that comes with being on the team.

It's like anything big in life that you acquire: a car, a home, insurance—you have to sign a contract that gives you parameters to work within. See, I ran my team as a business. And the business was to get them to the next level.

Since I was the basketball coach, everyone thought the "next level" was all about getting the kids into college as basketball players. And no question about it, that was important in the scope of what I was doing.

But in this case, the "next level" meant growing as young men, being responsible, respecting themselves and the community, taking pride in doing for others. That was the "next level" of life for those boys.

People talk about finding a better life, but you first must find a better minute and then a better hour and then a better day and a better week and a better month on up to a better year. It is a process that does not happen rapidly. There are incremental steps that lead to overall growth.

My players took those steps, and it shows up in the great fathers they have become.

And see, that's what leadership can do. It can make followers become leaders. That's the reality. Everyone can't be a leader at the same time; we would bump heads all day long. But you have to be a good follower to become a good leader.

More Than Just a Father

Chris Dixon was the toughest player I ever had. That kid was tough. And I'm tough. But I'm also an emotional coach. So I used to hug him. And at some point I stopped hugging him and he said, "Coach, you don't love us anymore?"

I asked, "Why would you say that?" He said, "Because you don't hug us anymore."

I was like, "Wow." That show of affection really mattered to him.

At the end of our practices, I used to take my son to the other end of the court and have some one-on-one instruction. Years later, Chris told me he was jealous of my time with my son because he never got that with his father.

But he also said, "You showed me how to be a good father." I tell you, that is the best thing I can hear from those young men. Above all, that is the most rewarding part of coaching—helping boys distinguish between being a father and being a dad.

At the conception of a child, a man technically becomes a "father." He contributed to the birth of a newborn and thereby earned that title. There are way too many "fathers" in the world and not enough dads.

A dad, I tried to instill in my players, was someone who took responsibility by being there for his child, providing financially and morally. Single moms have been incredible and, in some ways, the backbone of inner-city communities. My job was to arm my players with the strong reality that when the time came, they had to be "dads" and not just fathers.

That's what they have become, I'm proud to say. Those who have fathered children have been incredible, committed dads, which is critical.

On my team, only seven of the forty-five young men I coached had dads in the home.

Those are alarming numbers. And when you throw in the fact that sixty-five percent of the young boys in inner cities believe they will play some type of professional sports, then we are really talking about the value of preparing them for a harsh reality.

This is why leadership matters. Everyone cannot be a leader of others. And many do not realize they can lead themselves.

But once they experience leadership, they are then able to take ownership of their own lives and lead it where they want it to go, where it deserves to go.

The direction your life takes should be led by *you*! In the grand scheme of life, everyone can have leadership of his or her own life.

Everyone can, but not everyone does.

If your family is anything like mine, you have at least one relative that grown folks talk about with misguided admiration.

"Your cousin Michael is so smart and so talented. He can do anything he wants to do."

The problem is, Michael has not done much. He seemed smart enough and blessed with a particular skill set. He showed enough effort for his family to speak proudly about his potential. But Michael is twenty-nine years old and still has not distinguished himself as a professional beyond his family, which means he has underachieved.

But why?

As a kid growing up in McComb, Mississippi, that was a question that pricked my young brain: Why do some people achieve and others don't?

The question puzzled me for years. Finally, I understood.

The difference is distinctive: It's all in the way we think.

Receiving What You Deserve

We all are good at something, and yet all of us do not cultivate our strengths. Forget about weaknesses. Why waste time on weaknesses when we have strengths that we can build on?

I'm inspired each day by life. I'm blessed with the start of a new day, which is an opportunity to do something great. That's all about leading yourself to what you deserve. The way you think.

That's an important thing because life is less about wanting what you want and more about having a sense of accomplishment to desire what you *deserve* and the will to achieve it. If you work hard and put in the effort and extend yourself, you have earned the rewards of such a commitment. That's true whether you achieve your goals or not. But I believe you will find that with the proper mind-set and a commitment to put in the work, attaining the goals is realistic. It is important that you not let anyone tell you differently.

And that's all about how you think. Do you really

want more for yourself? Most people are complacent about life, unwilling to think beyond doing what they always have done.

It would be one thing if what you wanted rang your doorbell and waited for you to come outside to get it. But of course, it does not work that way.

The way it can work with gratifying results is to establish a mind-set of accomplishment, of success. *Do something.*

The first game I ever coached was my son Damien's team when he was in the fifth grade, in 1992. He was playing in a CYO (Catholic Youth Organization) league. I was content going to the games and seeing my son have fun playing basketball.

But one day the coach got into a car accident. They had lost the first five games, and the people drafted me out of the stands to take his place. "You were a star in high school and college—come on and coach these boys," they said.

There wasn't any room for me to refuse. We were about to play the No. 1 team. So I took those boys outside and found a flowerbed and put dirt on their faces. I said, "This is magic dirt. As long as you have this dirt on your faces, you can't be defeated."

And I got them all riled up and gave them a little instruction in the dirt outside, put them in certain positions on the court. When we came back into the gym, all the mothers called their boys over and had their handkerchiefs out. "Come here, baby," they said. "Let me get the dirt off."

I said, "No, let it alone, that's magic dirt." And the boys said, "Ma, Coach Carter said I should keep this on. It's magic dirt."

I told the kids, "If you can plant a seed in the ground and it grows beautiful like this rosebush here, if we put some of that on us, we're going to be like the rosebush."

So we went out and ended up winning the game by ten points. And one of the kids had never made a shot all year, not even in practice. He came down and threw up a shot from almost half court and it went in. And you could not tell him that wasn't the magic dirt working.

That was all about the way I think. Everybody needs something or someone to believe in. The only thing around was a flowerbed. I thought about that flowerbed and what it could mean for those growing children so quickly and so effectively that I taught myself something, which was great because I thrive on learning something new.

What I learned was this: If you plant a good seed in fertile ground, you're going to get something good from it. That's the way our lives are. Our lives are fertile, so it's all about what we plant in them. The universe doesn't care. It's going to give you back an abundance of whatever you plant.

There are Universal Laws that, in general, represent a set of principles that govern every aspect of the universe and are the means by which some believe our world and the entire cosmos continue to exist, thrive, and expand.

I have my own set of principles, which I call Coach Carter Laws:

- Law of Wisdom: We must use our experiences to build knowledge.
- Law of Harmony: We must get along with others.
- Law of Personal Evolution: We must understand our shortcomings and grow.
- Law of Free Will: We must take advantage of the opportunity to impact others.
- Law of Fellowship: We must respect the power of convening with friends.
- Law of Attraction: We must understand those people and/or things that appeal to us.
- Law of Unconditional Love: We must give love freely.
- Law of Divine Order: Some things are beyond your control.
- Law of Cause and Effect: We must understand the ramifications of our actions.
- Law of Compensation: Time is money.

COACH CARTER CARROT: THE NICKEL AND THE NAIL

As a kid, when I was able to earn a nickel, I would put a nail in my pocket with the nickel in there so they could rattle, make some noise. It was just a nickel's worth of money in my pocket, but it made me feel better psychologically because it sounded like more. Sometimes we just need something as a slump-buster to make us feel better.

We have to plant things in our fertile minds and bodies and let them grow in us to be successful.

Success many times is built on experiences. My players at Richmond High did not have many positive experiences on which to draw. In fact, most of those kids had never been outside Richmond, which meant their view of the world was foggy at best, totally distorted at worst.

So there were times when I would cancel practice and take them to Silicon Valley and meet millionaires. At that time, in 1999, my third year at Richmond High, Silicon Valley had two hundred millionaires per square mile. So it was fertile ground for my players to see living examples of wealth and potential.

We would ride out there—forty-five strong—and I would see a businessman on the street and introduce myself. I would let him know I had the freshmen, junior varsity, and varsity players from our school with me and we wanted to come in and see their offices and how they work. Or we would just show up at an office. No appointment. No warning. Just show up.

And I was never once turned down.

My thought process was simple: You sometimes have to see it to believe it.

Stepping Outside the Box

They saw the possibilities that lay ahead for them if they took the proper course and went about it the right way.

In fact, some of my players ended up having internships at those very companies we visited.

We also would visit Redwood National Park, where the bark literally is a deep red and the trees grow so huge you can actually drive a car through some. One of the kids said, "I didn't know there were forests here."

They learned that redwood trees grow as tall as three hundred feet and twenty feet in diameter—and that California is the only place in the world where they grow. It was an adventure to take them to that serene setting—something totally opposite the strife many of them faced daily at home.

In another way to relieve the players from what at times could be chaos in Richmond, I used to take the boys out for team dinners. At the first one, two kids picked up their steaks with their hands. They were used to everything they ate coming out of a fast-food bag. But we didn't laugh. We taught.

The next move was apparent to me: Set up etiquette classes for the boys. I wanted them to know how to comport themselves in particular situations. The classes were thorough and beneficial—and the players loved it. They learned about where the silverware should be placed on the table, the difference between a salad fork and a dinner fork, and so on—things they never knew mattered and things that would serve them well in the future.

All of this came down to one thing: The boys were underexposed. And if you're underexposed, then you are limited—in what you do and how you think. How could I, as a teacher and coach, allow them to stay unaware and uneducated? I couldn't.

So we got them exposed. I took them to San Francisco to work on the reelection campaign of former Mayor Willie Brown—another experience that had nothing to do directly with basketball but everything to do with life and the spirit of working together for a common cause.

Mayor Brown was the ideal figure for our kids to see. He was regal; when he walked into a room, all eyes were on him. His presence demanded your attention. I had this expression I used with our players: "If you're talking or thinking about talking, you're not listening."

But this was one time I did not have to worry. Not one of our kids said a word. They felt the magnitude of his presence. Everyone did.

He was bigger than the mayor of the largest city in Northern California. More than that, he showed everyone what success looked like.

He wore what had to be a tailor-made dark suit with a crisp, heavily starched white shirt that was monogrammed with his initials, elegant cuff links, a beautiful navy-and-red-striped necktie, and a pair of the most fashionable, shiny black shoes that likely came from an exclusive shop on Union Square in San Francisco. He topped his ensemble with a black fedora hat with a light brown, white, and red feather on the side.

Then there was Mr. James Brady, a technology executive who was a part of Mayor Brown's campaign. He was just as magnetic, but in a different way. Mr. Brady wore a button-down white silk shirt, black flowing slacks, and stylish black shoes. He sported an eye-catching watch, an understated gold necklace, and a pinky ring. He looked straight off the pages of *GQ* magazine. He was very subtle, but sharp, and you could tell he was an athlete in his day.

A very intelligent man, Mr. Brady spoke to our kids in a language they understood, and he and his wife, Deborah, were always there for us. Deborah Brady, in fact, gave our kids another perspective on success. Dressed elegantly in a beautiful dress, with complementary pearls around her neck, Mrs. Brady personified style, class, and status. She was perhaps the only female executive the boys had encountered at that point in their lives. Through her they received the first understanding that there are women of power, too.

So our kids were happy to work on the campaign, traveling through precincts distributing literature, and generally being a part of something special that they will remember all their lives.

Prior to that, we had juniors and seniors on our team who had never even been to San Francisco, which from Richmond is twenty minutes by car, thirty minutes by bus, thirty-five minutes by BART (the train system), and forty minutes by ferry. There were four ways to get there, but the kids did not know how—or even know to aspire to go anywhere at all.

From the Richmond shore, you can see the prodigious Golden Gate Bridge, the Bay Bridge, and the Richmond-San Rafael Bridge. And yet they seemed so far to our kids. They basically lived in a six- to seven-block radius in Richmond.

So, my job was more about teaching than coaching. We traveled with forty-five kids because there were fifteen players on all three levels of teams: varsity, junior varsity, and freshmen. If you were in our program, you were in our program.

The next year we had the team dinner, there were freshmen who picked up their steaks with their hands, and the two who had done it the previous year schooled those kids on what to do. That's why leadership is important—kids learn how to become leaders.

One of the things that really hurt me when I returned to Richmond High was the obvious lack of pride in the look of the building or hallways. The kids simply did not care how filthy or how much disarray it was in. They would be two feet from a trashcan and throw stuff on the floor. Two feet away.

The walls had graffiti on them. The bathrooms were just disgusting. There were leaks. It was a mess. As a test, I put a soda can on the floor in the boys' bathroom to see if anyone would pick it up.

The can stayed there for three weeks, which speaks to the lack of janitorial services and the students' disregard for the building.

I then had my players take on some responsibility for keeping the school in order. I assigned the freshmen team the front of the school, the junior varsity the middle of the school, and the varsity the back. They picked up trash and worked to keep things in order. They took on these assignments with pride—they enjoyed being leaders for the first time in their lives.

At the same time, I would not allow my players to take on that responsibility by themselves. The conditions were so bad at Richmond High that I knew something dramatic had to happen to get the attention of government to make much-needed changes.

So in 2000, I created "Scooting for Schools," an event where I traveled by scooter from Richmond to the state capital in Sacramento—a seventy-two-mile trek up Interstate 80 North. Now, this was not a motorized scooter. It was one of those scooters from your childhood, where you had one foot on the device and used the other to push off the ground to create momentum.

I could have come up with some other way to draw the attention of lawmakers, who needed to hear about the conditions of our school—and others—and do something about it. But I wanted to challenge myself. Also, I wanted to hammer home the point to my kids the importance of making a commitment and taking the initiative on important matters.

It was a grueling adventure, more difficult than I'd imagined. It took me three tough days to get there, but it was worth the effort.

My adventure became huge news. Media outlets from all over covered it—there was even a news helicopter that followed me some of the way—which was the best thing that could happen because it put pressure on legislators and a lot of kind, caring people learned about our plight.

I was just being me. A lot of people talked—or really, complained—about things. I did something. I started out at eight in the morning, before school. I slathered my feet in Vaseline to minimize blisters and donned thick socks and comfortable Nikes, black shorts, and a Richmond High sweatshirt. I also wore a helmet and pads. I was ready.

I started at the school, and my players and some students ran alongside me the first half mile or so before returning to school. Then, it was just me and the road—and a horde of media types that followed.

It was quite an ordeal. Many at school were taking odds that I would not make it. And truth be told, I had my questionable moments. For any age my journey would be a physical challenge. I was forty-three years old, making it a borderline insane attempt.

But I would not quit, despite the blisters on my feet and hands that came regardless of my preventive efforts, despite the fatigue, despite the pain. What kept me going? I was determined; the cause was so important. And I had to see it through for my players. If I quit, what kind of message would I have sent to them?

So I mentally overrode the obstacles. I called on that "don't quit" attitude I'd adopted as an athlete. I pushed on. My diet for the three days was hardly gourmet: Gatorade, Planter's Peanuts, Snickers, and M&Ms.

I lost ten pounds on the three-day odyssey, but I hardly eat like that today. In fact, I'm an advocate for healthy eating. I have a garden I maintain to produce fresh vegetables, and I'm a proponent of fighting the epidemic of childhood obesity. It was just that for the "Scooting for Schools," the physical demands did not allow me to sit down for the proper meals I truly enjoyed.

My goal on the scooter was to divide the trek into twenty-four miles a day, just two miles short of a marathon. With the media following in spurts, I took safe routes up or near Interstate 80 and slept in local hotels.

Along the way, I encountered hundreds of motorists and truckers who blew their horns or held signs to encourage me to keep pushing. The force of an eighteen-wheeler blew me into a ditch one day, but that did not break my spirit.

More times than not, my spirits were lifted by the people. People like Ms. Wilson, whom I met near Vallejo. She had spent forty-five years as a teacher and wanted to show her support for my mission.

So she waited two-and-a-half hours for me on the Interstate 80 frontage road to massage my hands and give me cookies and lemonade. That was such a nice gesture. She was a woman who cared about students and understood that the job of teaching is made far more difficult when educators have to contend with truly difficult conditions.

And that was what "Scooting for Schools" was all about: bettering conditions for our schools.

When I finally arrived in Sacramento, I was greeted by the city's fire department, which escorted me to the capitol. I had made it. It was an amazing feeling, a rewarding feeling.

There, I met for about an hour with a Richmond city

councilman and a school board member. We talked about making lawmakers aware of our plight, the condition of our schools, and how the district treated our students.

Before long, the contributions from people and companies came pouring in, like heavy rain. We ended up with donated computers and other materials that helped us gain some measure of decent working conditions.

I learned something quite valuable as I made that Richmond-to-Sacramento journey: People care.

If you are motivated by pure, honest, unselfish reasons, people will support you in every way possible. "Scooting for Schools" brought out people from all over who had no connection to Richmond or any other school existing in depraved conditions. They just cared enough to contribute big and small.

Ms. Wilson was the opposite of so many "teachers" already at Richmond High. It says a lot about a school and its academic commitment when there are several so-called educators with "emergency teaching credentials."

That was another way of saying they didn't know what they were doing and they did not care if they didn't know. I encountered so many teachers who would complain in the lounge about students' inability to learn, make jokes about it, but refuse to put forth the effort required to build kids up.

We literally had people at the school who didn't like kids. It was amazing in a horrible way. There were teachers who came to school with flip-flops on. We were supposed to be a tobacco-free school, and yet there were teachers smoking. It was just crazy and dysfunctional.

And it made for unnecessarily difficult teaching situations for the many teachers who did care. When you consider what role teachers play in a kid's life—students spend a large percentage of their time at school—you understand it is a huge responsibility.

And when you have that much responsibility, compensation should not be an issue. The way I see it, all teacher salaries should be doubled. Period. Everything we hope to become starts with a teacher. We need private and public education. You cannot have too many schools or too many teachers. And if we use what teachers get paid as a measuring stick, we must pay them better to attract some better minds.

At Richmond High, there came a point where the state government took over operation of the school. It was that bad.

With all this going on around us, we stayed our course. Our top two scorers from the previous year walked out when I distributed the player contracts. And yet we went on to win our first thirteen games of that first season, thereby making the players who remained bona fide celebrities.

The whole town embraced the players. In their small world, they were big stars.

And their stardom even impacted the more illicit part of living in Richmond. The players became the prey of local drug dealers, who believed they could "move more product" because of their popularity. So I had a real battle all the time and from all different directions.

One of the more prolific drug dealers in Richmond came to visit me at my sporting goods store at the height of our success. He told me that he provided a service to the community just like I was in helping my players.

He said, "I won't mess with your players because they are doing great things. But if they slip up, they're mine." He was not joking, and I took him completely seriously.

So I had to make sure my kids had traction.

And I had to keep my traction as well. But I was anchored in one fundamental belief: Giving starts the receiving.

A lot of people believe you give and then it is gone. Oh, no, no, no.

It is a universal law. You give unconditionally, expecting nothing in return, and your receiving will be bountiful. I believe that. I'm living proof of that.

When you are a leader or even a good listener, you have to make the decision with confidence and go for it, understanding that others are watching and can and should learn from your leadership.

Chapter Two

Start Your Day with the "Write" Stuff

Most of my life I have owned my own business. However, I did work for a short time in corporate America. How that transpired speaks to the power of a personal practice that I complete on a daily basis: writing down my ambitions. There is power in seeing your goals on paper; it propels you to pursue them with unwavering commitment.

I needed a job at twenty-two, directly after college, and read an advertisement in a local Bay Area newspaper about job openings at Osborne/McGraw-Hill. I called and set up an interview with the person in charge. I got there for my interview, and there was a long line of people outside seeking employment at this hot, upstart company in Berkeley, California, which was growing fast.

I bypassed the line with my résumé in hand and

somehow ended up speaking to the man who was hiring. He didn't know I was there looking for a job.

He said, "What company are you representing?"

I said, "Myself. I'm here to start my career."

He said, "Really? Well, young man, you're going to have to get in line with the others."

I said, "You think I want to stand in line?"

He said, "That's pretty creative, young man."

And then he hired me on the spot. I got that job because I went there to *get* a job, not apply for one. That was my written-down goal for that day, and seeing it helped me believe I would achieve it.

When we see our objectives on paper, it allows us to visualize fulfilling the objective, which signifies success. For reasons big and small, it is imperative to write down information, thoughts, ideas, and goals.

When I eat out at restaurants nowadays, I often wonder why the servers many times do not use a little pad to jot down the orders for the table. Inevitably, no matter how strong a memory he or she might have, something is forgotten.

It is not surprising; it's human nature. People forget things. The surprise comes when a person does *not* forget something. And it confirms my belief that too many people do not understand the power of writing stuff down. Too many people do not realize that the shortest pencil has better recall than the longest memory.

It is one of the more practical principles of achievement, and yet writing down your thoughts and goals is one of the least used among people. *Write it down.*

Whether it is the grocery list, the day's chores, or your life's ambitions...seeing them on paper equates to getting them done.

Studies have indicated that we are *ten times* more likely to get something done if we write it down. I like to think of it as your road map or GPS to success. It keeps you organized and headed in the right direction to reach your desired destination.

Writing down my responsibilities and goals and most everything else has been a practice of mine for about three decades. It really became a way of life in college. Things were more difficult in the classroom being in competition with the best of the best. Things were more challenging in life, being away from home and having the entire responsibility for my success or failure. And I was always involved in so many things that my cup ranneth over with commitments.

Having something on paper as a guide helped me keep things in order, which helped me function much more efficiently. After all, a goal is nothing more than a great idea with a deadline.

I have carried that disposition with me much of my life. As a basketball coach, I was extremely organized. Our practices were all laid out on paper, everything down to the minute.

The practice schedule for that day was posted on a wall, and that gave the players a sense of organization. I would put time on the clock and they knew what station to get to next based on the time. It made for efficient and productive practices. Seeing the practice schedule in writing helped them understand what we were attempting to accomplish that day.

Also, I would scout our upcoming opponent and break down its players, team strengths and weaknesses...every detail that was important to how we played against them. Seeing that information on paper allowed our kids to study it and get it into their mind for that game.

A Life Game Plan

Just as you have a game plan in sports, you must have one in life. There has to be order, and writing down information promotes just that.

People would be surprised at how much more they would get done in adhering to this simple but significant ideal. Establishing order in your daily life through writing down your thoughts and goals helps bring the kind of clarity in your ambitions that you just cannot get from storing them only in your mind.

The results would be immediate and unmistakable. It is easy to identify achievement. And I do not buy into the notion that people "overachieved" when they reach their goal. Overachieve? No, you just did what was already in you. You applied yourself one hundred percent, and you got out of it what you put into it.

All you can put in is one hundred percent. What is one hundred and ten percent? That is overstating what can be done. Once you give your all, there is not another ten percent to give.

Here's what's funny: This writing thing is not a new idea. Think about it: Six thousand years ago, cavemen were writing on walls, communicating, plotting their course. The Neanderthal man, for instance, identified the animals that were prey and the animals Neanderthals would need to stay clear of. So he would draw a line and draw images of what animals they could eat on one side and what animals could eat them on the other.

Images were written on walls to communicate clearly and to emphasize the point. I go to bed every night with a pen, a pad, and a tall glass of water on my nightstand. I drink the water to purify my body and then I write down my goals for the next day. It is almost liberating to see on paper a checklist of responsibilities. I wake up eager to start the new day.

If you have to go to the grocery store and then to the cleaners and then to the pharmacy and then to the mall and then to pick up a cake from the bakery and then to your sister's house to drop off her mail...if all that is bunched up in your brain, one or two things are inevitable: You will forget one of the tasks; or most likely they will be crashing around in your head so much that they will exhaust you and you'll say, "Forget it. I'm not doing all that."

Contrast that to writing those same daily goals down and then—and this is key—prioritizing them, which means putting them in order of importance and then going down the list. It seems much less daunting then; in fact, it becomes something quite achievable, and you get excited as you cross off one completed chore after the next.

In the land of the blind, a one-eyed man is king. Why? Because he can see.

Think about a wedding planner. He or she will ask the client every conceivable question about the occasion—how many guests, what kind of flowers, what color schemes, what kind of chairs, inside or outside, and so forth—to get every detail for that event. It would all be written down. Seeing it allows the wedding planner to attack the job with precision and purpose.

Also, writing things down is like an insurance policy. Just in case you get off track, you have something to refer to, a security blanket of sorts that keeps you in the moment.

Advancing the Plan

I started that corporate job in the mailroom. Within one year, I was promoted to assistant manager in marketing. Why? It was my willingness to learn. I had written down my goals and could see where I wanted to go. That made it clear for me. I advanced because I was doing more than I was paid to do. I used my own money to attend courses and conferences that gave me specialized information. I showed that I wanted to advance.

It boggled the minds of coworkers that I would get the promotion over others with more experience.

Here's the thing: The promotion did not mean I was smarter than them. It meant I knew more about that job.

In other words, I was inspired. Not motivated. We do not need motivation. We need inspiration, which is different.

Motivation comes through inspiration. Inspiration comes through an action step. *Inspiration and motivation are brother and sister.* They are connected.

Motivation is a reason to act. Inspiration is a state of mind, a state of being that allows you to take an action step on all things that will advance your business or your life.

As a coach, I never tried to motivate my team. Motivation comes and goes. I always looked to inspire my players to seek their best effort on the court, in the classroom, at home, everywhere, and at all times. That philosophy made it easy for them to be ready to play a basketball game and to grow in their lives. They were inspired people.

As inspired people, we take that extra class. We show up for work early and stay late. We read that extra book. We do all that not because someone motivated us to do it. We do it because we are inspired by success and achievement.

I had moments as an athlete when I was so exhausted that I didn't think I could take another step. But I always pushed my way through because I was inspired to accomplish the goal. Inspiration was in my DNA.

Eyes on the Prize

When you're challenged, you can sometimes lose focus. It becomes more difficult to stay the course. Most people cannot stay on task, especially when there is pressure or a real challenge. ADD is a prominent condition among people under duress.

And I don't mean attention deficit disorder. I mean *Always Doing Damage.* So many of us cannot get out of our own way. We do damage to our potential either by not outlining our goals by writing them down or by straying from the plan when a challenge arises.

How many people do you know who tell you about their plan and how they are all excited about it at the start? Then something comes along that makes achieving the goal more difficult. It is then when ADD kicks in. Instead of hunkering down and preparing to battle, they jump out of the boat and seek something else, doing damage to their own dreams.

At the first sign of adversity, they quit. All the loser excuses come out: "This is not for me." "My boss doesn't like me." And on and on...

If you are in a position you don't like, the only way to get out of it is to work your way out of it. You can't wish your way out or buy your way out or complain your way out of it.

Let's say, for argument's sake, that the challenge was so severe that you abandoned your ambition. But maybe, just maybe, if some persistence had kicked in, the challenge could have been overcome. You confront a challenge with a purpose.

It's the same old learning how to ride a bike mentality. Many kids get on a bicycle and fall. Some get up and put the bike in the house; they didn't like how it felt to fall, and even though they got up with no bruises, they are afraid they may fall again.

Others get back on that bike and continue working at it until they ride on their own.

A lot of times it is willpower, too. *Persistence and willpower are like brothers.* They go together. You have one, you have the other. Together, they are a force.

When I locked out my team from the gym, the naysayers were all over the place. There were some supporters, definitely. But because the team had galvanized the community, I heard some really nasty things from a lot of people who wanted my head.

But I'm nothing if not persistent. I believed in what I was doing, so when I was challenged, my willpower kicked in. I would not budge. I stayed the course. And the end result was beautiful.

Ask anyone who did not succumb to adversity about how they felt in making it happen. I can answer for them: exhilarated and accomplished—just like the kid who kept getting on the bicycle and finally learned how to ride it without training wheels.

It totally changes your life. Achieving brings the kind of fulfillment that breeds more successes. Some of us who failed in a business venture did not lose that determination and found success the next time, like the kid who fell off the bicycle but got right back on it. That's persistence.

Nothing can be done without persistence because adversity will come. It is just a matter of how you deal with it.

Persistence is much stronger and more rewarding than failure could ever be depressing. Persistence overcomes failure and brings a powerful reward.

So, we have to cultivate persistence to where it becomes a part of our DNA. Like the redwood trees, if you aerate your ground, put fertilizer down, and plant good seeds, you will grow a persistent nature.

People say, "Man, I really want a harvest." I say, "Well, you really need to get to planting."

The problem is, most people are not truly interested in growing. They seek a path of least resistance. The perceived easy way out. Sometimes, though, that path leads to a minefield. Sometimes there is no escalator or elevator. What happens then? You take the stairs, one

COACH CARTER CARROT

Redwood trees start with a very small seed but grow as high as three hundred feet. A tree will grow in the direction the twig is bent. In other words, if you plant positive elements in your life and stretch them toward your goals, you can direct it wherever you'd like it to grow.

foot in front of the other. That's how you get it done: Define a purpose. That's how you develop persistence. Write it down. Put it in your heart.

Wishing for good things to happen provides nothing. Wishing with no action gets you on a treadmill of failure and nonfulfillment. Running in place. Hustling backward.

But there is also a treadmill of success. One of my seven sisters, Diane, once bought a weight-loss gadget off one of those infomercials on late-night TV. A few weeks later, she received it and went on to lose fifteen pounds and kept it off. She was persistent about achieving her goal. She had a class reunion to attend and was inspired to show up thirty pounds lighter. And she did.

That's the power of inspiration. She walked the treadmill of success, repeating those things that brought her to her desired goal. In her case, she had a class reunion to attend and she wanted to look her best. Whatever the inspiration, if you get on a treadmill of success, that goal is attainable.

Specializing in Specialized Information

I keep my work area very clean and neat, whether at an office or at home. I am organized.

But organization does not look the same to all people. Some people can have a cluttered desk and find all the papers they need. They have their own "system."

The problem is, that kind of disorder can only last

for so long. It will not hold up in the long haul. At some point, it will break down.

Then what do you do? That is when I think it necessary to talk to yourself. Some people joke that it is okay to talk to yourself as long as you don't answer yourself.

I say it is healthy to debate with yourself either way. It is like playing chess against yourself. You make a move and then you go to the other side of the table and examine the board and go, "Oh, I see what he's doing." And now you think of how to counter that move.

That's how you gauge your life. Some things you strongly believe in. No matter what political side you are on or what religion, if you practice and pray, you will be all right.

We enrich our country with constructive debate, and that debate starts with yourself. When one part of your brain says you have a great idea, the other part of your brain should reinforce that notion. It charges your mind to go through all kinds of scenarios and circumstances and perspectives. It helps to fully flesh out an idea or a goal.

Then, with that full concept, we can give ourselves a profound gift: We educate ourselves. This does not mean going back to school for another degree, which is never a bad thing because you can never be overeducated.

It means we have the most comprehensive resource ever created at our fingertips: the Internet. On a computer, we can seek and find whatever specific information we desire toward our goals. The Internet provides limitless information that can give us an abundance of whatever we seek.

We have the tools now that man never envisioned. But you have to know what to seek.

So the question is: What are we searching for?

Outside of our specific goals, there should be a search of knowledge of self. It might sound trite, but if we know where we come from, it helps guide us to where we're going. It adds a sense of security.

We have to read history. We have to understand geography. We have to speak proper English. We have to know mathematics. We have to know our roots.

This is all stuff we can control. But it goes back to how we think: You cannot be a master of your own destiny if you're not a thinker. Thoughts create the words that we speak, and words are impregnated with actions. Bear these important points in mind:

Continue to write down your thoughts and plans. Seeing your ambitions on paper gives you the structure to execute your goals. Seeing it is believing it.

Be inspired. From within has to come the charge to do something. It has to be a part of your makeup.

Be persistent. If you want something badly enough, no obstacle will sidetrack you. You will avoid the minefields and replenish the mind and stay on course.

All of that we can control.

The only thing you do not have control over is time. Once it ticks off the clock, it is gone. Once it's lost, it can never to be recaptured. We can't manipulate time.

And so that makes time our most valuable resource.

It is all about how we use it. Think about it: In every breath we take, we're getting closer to leaving this life. The clock starts ticking at birth. We do not know when it will run out for us, which makes it so precious.

My record as a basketball coach was great. We won seven championships and many tournaments, and so forth. But it was even better than that because while the scoreboard said we lost some games, theoretically, I have never lost a basketball game—the time just keeps running out on the clock. When it reads all zeroes after the fourth quarter, there are times when the other team has more points than us at that moment, denoting them the winner. But I keep on playing. Tomorrow brings a new day. If we can change our attitudes on how we function from day to day, our lives can be totally different.

And that thinking has to be about using our time for achievement. Mediocrity does not serve us well. Poor choices do not serve us well. Our time has to be about high achievement.

Sometimes our success is based simply on our choices. A wrong or bad choice can ruin your life, take you way off course, waste your time.

But here's the thing: Everything is connected. If we think things through, think about the way to success, then we create a solid action plan and make decisions that benefit us. We do not spend time on that treadmill to nowhere, where so many people reside.

That's where the negative energy comes in. Those on that treadmill can hardly find the good in anything.

They gripe and complain about one thing or another, so much so that they are hard to be around. That's the quickest way to get rid of all your friends and to get your future canceled. No one wants to be around someone with a cloud of negativity hovering over him.

But that treadmill works the other way, too, a treadmill of success. On it, you develop strong habits that stand up no matter what the venture, no matter what the goal. Just like people make a habit out of being negative and being unable to persist in times where persistence is necessary, you can also make a habit of being upbeat, of being someone always searching for the optimistic view.

If all things positive are a part of your makeup, that bright perspective helps you execute your duties with a commitment and a focus that are unwavering. Success then becomes a habit, a way of life. It becomes about demanding excellence.

The Balance of Power

You cannot have a good business life if you do not have a good personal life. They go hand in hand, a counterweight to the other.

If you've flown on a small plane before, often the flight attendant will ask passengers to move from one side of the plane to the other so there will be equal passengers on both sides, giving the plane balance.

There should be the same idea about life.

As much as we demand success in business, we have to demand it in the way we live.

You have to catch a flight, and you know, based on parking your car, checking your bag, and getting through security, that you should arrive about two hours before takeoff to get yourself situated.

But you cannot go to the airport and not see dozens of people all day running through the terminals like maniacs, desperate to arrive at the gate in enough time to catch their flight. Why does this repeatedly happen? Because so many people constantly try to push that envelope. They try to squeeze in another phone call or another chore, putting immense stress on themselves to make their flight.

Meanwhile, if you don't make that flight, it is easy to find the person at fault: *you*. And you have no one else to blame.

Repeatedly putting yourself in a vulnerable position is not living right. In our minds, we have to realize the whole world does not revolve around us. There are rules to follow. If that is understood at a young age, it becomes a part of your makeup, and your thinking and behavior will reflect that knowledge.

When I was a kid growing up in Mississippi, my mother was a domestic, and I was the only one of her nine children that she could take to jobs with her. She knew she could sit me in a particular place, give me some toys, and I would not stray from that area. I would sit there and not be a bother to her.

That ability to focus on one thing at a time is a part of me to this very day.

Conscious Versus Self-Conscious

It is okay and even important to be a conscious, aware person because it means you are embracing that which is around you in a positive way.

A conscious person dresses the best he or she can, looks the best, smells the best. You can control that, and that is your presentation to the world. You can look at someone and say, "I know he feels good; look at how he's dressed."

When I see a nicely dressed person, I'm not afraid to tell him or her, "You look good." That person took the time and planning to put together a nice outfit; that person deserves the compliment.

That's no different from putting together a business plan. Your presentation, how you come off when someone looks at you, is extremely important in your mission.

Think about this: You go into a very clean bathroom at a restaurant, and you remember it. You remember it positively, as something that is not the norm. That impression you get from that bathroom impacts whether you will do business there.

That's what the conscious person will consider.

Now, think about this: McDonald's is great, but it does

not make the best burger in world. Still, it sells more burgers than anyone else. Why? Well, you could argue McDonald's is in the real estate business.

The sign out front tells you that they have sold billions. To sell that many burgers, you have to have outlets, and McDonald's has them. There are probably two or three new McDonald's opened every day. They are everywhere; they are in our consciousness.

When I was a kid, going to McDonald's was a huge treat. It was like going out to a really nice restaurant now. As you get older, you go more often because you can afford it. And you become a parent and you take your kids there, too. So McDonald's ends up staying with you, in your consciousness your entire life.

Ronald McDonald is probably the most recognizable mascot in the world. Kids, parents, grandparents, and even great-grandparents know who he is. We are all conscious of that.

A self-conscious person thinks differently from a conscious person. He or she thinks: What's in it for me?

That person is conscious of only himself. You could bring up something that happened to you and the self-conscious person would respond by how what you said related to him.

Example: A guy says to a friend, "I'm going to Las Vegas for the weekend to celebrate my anniversary with my wife. We've been married two great years."

The self-conscious person responds: "I don't like Vegas. Last time I was there, I lost five hundred dollars."

A conscious person would have responded: "Oh,

that's great. Congratulations on the anniversary. You should have a great time in Vegas."

The self-conscious person's unspoken mantra: What's in it for me?

When people are so self-conscious, they can look in the mirror and actually see their very best friend or their worse enemy. Some people cannot get out of their own way with negative thoughts.

I have been around family or friends who have the gift of gab, look good, etc. But their life has not come together. And all the symptoms of failure are there: late, unorganized, no well-defined plan, an array of problems, a negative attitude, little interest in acquiring knowledge, not accountable. It shows in their overall being. "I just can't get a break," they say.

Well, all circumstances are not tailor-made for us. We have to tailor our life to what the opportunities are.

Business is business; deals are made to benefit all parties involved. But a self-conscious person will complicate a deal because he doesn't think he's receiving enough of the pie. And that position would not be about business. It would be about him and his insecurities.

That is what it boils down to—being devoid of security within. The attention or subject always has to be on the self-conscious person, or he or she will immediately feel neglected.

And in business and in life, that self-conscious person does not find a comfort level to reside in.

The universe responds to what you deserve, not what you need or want. So many people cannot be happy because they live in the lane of "I want more" instead of *deserving* more because they put the work in.

The Business of Hard Work

Early in my life, when I was not even a teenager, I found myself around entrepreneurs. Some were good businessmen, some not so good.

But they all had one common trait: They all worked hard. They all planned and knew what their profit margins were and remained flexible. They had habits, good, strong habits that are critical to business.

If the sign said they were open at eight in the morning, they were there. That is an invaluable part of business and life—doing what you say you're going to do.

In fact, I believe the best businessmen underpromise and overdeliver. In other words, never promise more than you can deliver. Worse, never deliver less than promised. Both positions mean the same thing: Deliver!!!

Delivering is something quite different from wishing to deliver. People love wishing, as in, "I wish I were successful." Or, "I wish I would get promoted."

That's not going to get it done. It takes some will and planning and execution to make it happen, to deliver you where you want to be.

This is the greatest time in the history of mankind. Now more than ever, education, power, products, intellectual properties are accessible. If you don't have your share or what you deserve, whose fault is it?

I have heard from people: "Why are you working so much tonight?"

My answer: "Because I don't want it on my desk tomorrow."

A Single-Minded Focus

Thomas Edison—get this—failed at creating the light-bulb *thousands of* times. That is not a misprint. He could not get it right, but he was undeterred.

How could he remain so steadfast after so many failures? He was a man of only three months' formal education. That is not a misprint, either. But he had a single-minded focus that pulled him through.

Simply, he would not quit. He wrote down his ambitions. He had a defined goal and he was persistent. And he achieved his mission, establishing himself as a historic figure.

Henry Ford's story was similar to Mr. Edison's. Mr. Ford had just a sixth-grade education. But he had a vision of creating the nation's first car. It was not easy. There were road blocks; for years he could not figure out how to create the car in his imagination. But there was nothing that quelled his persistence and willpower.

And in 1908, Mr. Ford produced the Model T, marking the beginning of the Motor Age and, essentially, changing America.

These are extreme examples of what can be done with the right mind, attitude, persistence, and talent. But if they could do what they did in their time, imagine what any of us could do now, with unlimited resources and access.

To advance that point, Mr. Ford also understood the value of "purchasing knowledge," meaning when he could not figure out a particular detail, he hired someone who could. And it pays to know when and where to purchase knowledge.

Competitive Edge

It is a different day. The consumer always should have been king, but that was not always the case.

In the 1970s, '80s, and '90s I can remember catching the bus and the drivers were just as rude as they could be. I recall walking in businesses like the bank or even the grocery store and being ignored by all the workers.

Well, it is a different day now because competition is aplenty, and businesses are competing more than ever for the hard-to-get dollar.

Now, the gruff bus drivers are some of the nicest people in the world. There are "greeters" at department stores and banks—someone who stands there with the specific job of welcoming customers into the establishment.

And when you depart, they leave you with, "Thanks for coming. Have a great day."

Good business dictates that you essentially form a partnership with the business that walks through your door.

Catch a taxi to the airport and the driver not only is pleasant, but before you get out, he asks: "When are you coming back? I will come pick you up."

That never would have happened just a few years ago. Now, employees are like partners for a company. Their presence and disposition impact how consumers view the overall business. Customer service is king. And society is now full of specialists.

In football, the kicker handles one special job. In basketball, you often have players who are designated defenders. In baseball, there is the closer who comes out of the bullpen to do one job.

Everyone plays his position to get the job done. It's that way in business now more than ever.

These companies are the same ones I implored my students to explore after college. There are less than five thousand jobs in professional sports, which means a whole lot of kids hold on to far-fetched dreams.

I let my players know that a company like Microsoft had more than ten thousand millionaires working at that one company alone.

It was one of many examples I gave them on how they could be successful outside of athletics.

As people, we have to be like water. Water can be manifested in steam, snow, ice, mist, rain. That's how we have to be in our lives—flexible.

Chapter Three

Education Comes in Many Forms

When I was in high school, I played varsity basketball and baseball, and flourished at both sports. One of the perks of such prowess was to wear a letterman's jacket around school.

After getting enough money to buy one, I went to the local sporting goods store to make the purchase. I was so excited. What I got instead was the inspiration to start my own sporting goods store one day.

It was not because I had such a wonderful experience. It was the opposite: I had a horrific time.

The owner of the store did not value my business. He was rude, impatient, and racist. Ultimately he was so harsh and insensitive that he drove me to tears.

I had never experienced an adult so mean and hateful. But that searing experience actually inspired my interest in opening a sporting goods store, even though

I did not know a thing about running a business. I left that store without my letterman's jacket. But I promised him before I departed that one day I would open a competitive store and put his store out of business.

I went on to college a few years later and studied business administration. With that awful experience still in my mind, I created a special study project with my business professor in which I built up a model sporting goods store and ran it from the ground up, learning all about inventory, marketing, customer service, and everything else involved in sustaining a business.

When I returned to Richmond, I used the knowledge I had gained to start my own sporting goods store, just around the corner from the store belonging to the man who treated me so awfully. And five years later, just as I had promised him before leaving his store, that man was out of business.

I ended up owning the entire block of the businesses with a barbershop and hair salon along with the sporting goods store—all before I took the coaching job at Richmond High.

I was not inspired to have a successful store that ended up running that man out of business because of his mistreatment of me when I was in high school. Rather, I was successful because I learned from a number of sources.

I learned from college and from my own experiences as well as from his mistakes. That's the beauty of self-education: There are an infinite number of ways to absorb information to improve yourself and your work life.

Eat. Love. Learn.

The smartest people in the world got that way because they have a passion for knowledge. They crave it, breathe it, ingest it. And we know knowledge is king.

I love to learn. Anything. Everything. If it's something I don't know, I want to know about it. And if there is something I already know, then I want to learn more. I have an insatiable curiosity about all forms of human endeavor and life in general. Everything in this world fills me with wonder and a sense of wanting to know more.

Of course, I wasn't born this way. Once again, I credit my parents for instilling in me this love of learning from my earliest days.

At school, my teachers reinforced this mind-set. The first moment I walked into a library, I was hooked on books. At home, I always have a book on my nightstand, along with a pen and pad and glass of water.

Not a night goes by that I do not add to my depth and breadth of understanding and knowledge. If I could, I would devour every ounce of information this world has to offer!

The benefit of this is clear: When you are armed with knowledge, your sense of self-worth, confidence, and certainty increase. You understand the challenges and you are prepared to take them on.

A love of learning not only will make you relentless at the art of self-improvement, but will provide learning in you that adds to the depth of your being.

To achieve any goal you set in life, you must lay the groundwork, and that groundwork always involves learning something new. You can never be too much of an "expert" at anything; it's always possible to learn something.

You have heard the stories of how much work Michael Jordan or Larry Bird or Magic Johnson put into their game, even though they had reached the pinnacle of their profession. You think Bill Gates does not continue to bombard his brain with new information even as he is an iconic figure with Microsoft?

Advanced education is a must for doctors, teachers, construction workers...any profession. Attorneys have to learn new laws and how they apply to specific cases. A mechanic's job is ever-evolving as new engines are built. In every walk of the working life, there are needs to learn more and more—even after you have mastered a particular discipline.

With the economic crisis of recent years, many Americans have had to abandon a career they were well versed in and transition into something totally new just to have a job. Some of the changes have been radical—accountants becoming teachers, teachers becoming cashiers, etc. It has required change, which in turn, requires an education to acquire a new skill set.

My first *real* job was working as a janitor at a grocery store when I was fourteen. It was at Cartwright's Grocery in Richmond and the owner ran the business with an iron fist. He was stern but fair, a true businessman.

He treated customers well. His inventory was extremely

well stocked. For an independent neighborhood store of about four thousand square feet, it was incredible. He had meats, produce, household items, and canned foods. Mr. Cartwright did not have just one brand. If you wanted a can of beans, he had a variety of brands.

He started his business in the basement of his home and grew to the grocery store and then to where he owned all four businesses at one intersection. A graduate of Grambling University, he was a self-made man who inspired me even more so than the man who treated me so badly.

I knew from Mr. Cartwright's constant and huge repeat business that he valued his customers' money and support.

Working under Mr. Cartwright, I was eager to learn about all aspects of the job. Before long, I advanced to baggage clerk, then to checkout clerk, and finally junior assistant manager—all in just one year.

I was so committed that the manager never had to ask me to learn something new; I was the one demanding knowledge from day one.

Here's another example of where an unbridled love of learning can lead:

Obviously, having a personal stake in the outcome plays an enormous role in building and cultivating a love of learning. There is no substitute for enthusiasm about learning and life. When I was trying to teach my ballplayers about the impact of government in their lives by having them work on San Francisco Mayor Willie Brown's campaign, they took a personal stake in the election.

And because they did, they worked enthusiastically. After the election, their civics teacher told me that she had never experienced such an enthusiastic group of young men so excited about learning. They were able to apply the lessons of the classroom to real life, and each of them had gained a stake in learning about their subject.

Hollywood Highlights

When I went to Hollywood for the production of *Coach Carter*, I had an opportunity to spend a considerable amount of time with the producers of the film, Mike Tollin and Brian Robbins. These producers are among the best in the business, having produced films such as *Varsity Blues* and television shows such as *Smallville*.

Rather than wasting my time hanging out on the movie set all day, I instead followed my love of learning and spent as much time with the producers as I could. As a result, even though I had not planned on a career in the movie business, I learned a considerable amount of information about how that business works, and I have become a producer and a writer.

I discovered that I had acquired the skills required for a new business venture. One day, I hope to produce my own television shows and movies, and it will have been my love of learning which gave me the inspiration and head start.

Positive Self-Image

A positive self-image is the foundation for all success. You cannot succeed at any endeavor unless you are first convinced that you *can* succeed. Too many people fail in their tasks more from a lack of belief in themselves than they do from a lack of competence. All the aptitude in the world will not serve you if you do not have the right attitude to fortify your skill set.

Some do not have a positive self-image because they have not identified what it is. Moreover, it is not easy to identify, especially when your surroundings do not promote such feelings.

You can look at positive self-image like this: A kitten looks into a mirror and sees a lion staring back at him. You can also call it an article of faith in oneself, the belief that one can accomplish any task if one is willing to invest the right amount of time and effort. Positive self-image is the steel that fortifies your backbone whenever you try to lift a heavy load and carry it on your shoulders. It is being and staying positive; you will amaze yourself with what you can accomplish.

I acquired a positive self-image mainly from my parents and older siblings, who never failed to praise me and give me positive reinforcement whenever I accomplished a goal, whether it was in sports or in the classroom. My mother always took time out to make sure that I finished my homework. She would check up on me at school to make sure that I obeyed and respected my teachers and paid attention in class.

As a result, I achieved good grades, and she was the first to give me words of praise and to instill the pride of accomplishment in me. Through my mother's efforts, I learned the connection between hard work and accomplishment, and through my accomplishments I garnered a positive self-image.

When I first met my players at Richmond High School, I realized that most of them were suffering from poor self-image. Many came from broken homes and lacked that parental figure that could offer them encouragement and positive reinforcement. As the head basketball coach, I also undertook the roles of mentor, role model, and parent.

When one of my players needed advice on a personal matter, I made myself available to him. The reasons were twofold: First and foremost, I cared. Second, I wanted him to take a positive approach to any situation.

I talked to my players about peer pressure, girlfriend pregnancy, gangs—the subjects were endless. Each discussion ended with me emphasizing positive solutions, as the job daily was to build self-esteem as much as it was coaching basketball.

When my players achieved success on the court, I was there to offer them praise and instill self-confidence. I hugged them and slapped "five" with them and punctuated their efforts with uplifting compliments. They deserved the support and I knew it would inspire good feelings about themselves, which was critical to their functioning as positive people.

Visualization Has Its Place

Before you undertake any task, it is important to take some quiet moments and see yourself achieving your goal. This is not daydreaming. It's called visualization, and it is a critical part of cultivating a positive self-image.

Imagining yourself accomplishing the task puts you in the place of actually doing it and allows you to move forward confident it can be done because you've already seen it. It makes the follow-through feel much more attainable.

This is a technique I learned early in life from sports and carried into other aspects of my life. For example, shooting free throws is a task that requires intense concentration and self-control. It is an unguarded shot, but many times players are not proficient from the foul line because they do not provide themselves with the positive reinforcement of visualization.

I made more than ninety percent of my free throws in high school and college not only because I was a naturally gifted shooter. A big part of my accuracy was my routine of actually visualizing the ball going into the basket before I shot it.

I established my preshot routine, setting up with the proper balance, establishing a smooth rhythm with four bounces, and then releasing the ball with the same degree of force and spin each time.

I'm clear on this: If I did not see the ball going into

the basket in my preshot routine, I would not have been as effective as a shooter.

The impact of visualization extends far beyond the basketball court. When I decided to make my life story into a movie, visualization was critical in its execution.

I had to meet with top executives from Paramount Pictures to pitch the idea of my story becoming a film. Because I had not tried to sell a movie before, I was afflicted with doubts as to whether I could convince the powers-that-be to green light my idea.

So I turned to my old friend, visualization. I practiced telling the story of my life over and over in front of a mirror. Then I called a friend of mine, a Hollywood screenwriter, and practiced telling him the story of my life as it would play as a movie. The more I did it, the more comfortable I became.

When my friend was convinced, I knew that I was ready to take the next step and meet with Paramount. In our meeting, the words rolled out of me just as they had in my visualizations and practice sessions with my friend, and I could tell that I immediately earned the executives' attention.

It took only forty-eight hours after our meeting for them to approve making *Coach Carter*.

The reward of a positive self-image is accomplishment. That is the entire point of having a positive self-image—to achieve the mission.

When my older brother, Junior, taught me to play basketball, he always took time to praise me. When I used proper form in shooting the ball, I earned a "good job" from my brother. I came to hunger for his approval, so I worked hard to get better and better—just to hear a laudatory remark from Junior.

Success builds on itself, and by succeeding at many smaller tasks, I set myself up to succeed at the biggest goals, thereby building my positive self-image. But I visualized it all before it happened.

With my Richmond High players, I got them in the mode of believing the success they wanted could be accomplished and to sit back in quiet moments and see themselves making plays, see themselves celebrating victory.

This was really significant there because there was hardly anything positive at school, at home, or in the community for the kids to embrace. But when they started to embrace their own successes and to see their successes before they even happened, their spirits were exponentially lifted.

COACH CARTER CARROT

People with a job hit the snooze button on the alarm clock over and over in the morning. They walk with their heads down. People with a career get up in the morning eager to start a new day. They walk with their heads up so they can see where they're going. And they're ready to take chances, ready to get going.

Self-Discipline's Value

One of the toughest things to do is to discipline your-self. That is why weight-loss programs remain in such prominence—people cannot get a hold of themselves.

That's called self-discipline, or a lack thereof. The ability to motivate oneself regardless of outside factors—that's self-discipline, and it is paramount to success in business and in life.

It is one thing to have a job and to follow your boss's instructions. That is something all of us can do, though some of us do it better than others. But self-discipline requires something extraordinary.

It requires a dedication to your duty as set by you, for yourself, in accordance with your own standards.

Self-discipline means being your own boss within the job that you have. Without it, achieving the desired level of success becomes much more difficult.

Why? Because our impulses tell us to go home and rest, to play a round of golf, to attend a social event when there is work to be done. It is a natural thing. But self-discipline forces us to understand that those occa-sions that really are wants and not needs will be there after the job is done, too.

Those who get ahead, who are consistent achievers, are able to sacrifice the social activity to assure the work is complete at the highest standard.

Exercising self-discipline increases the possibility of successful outcomes in all phases of life and work. You can believe there were many nights when the world's top businessmen had chances to attend a ball or simply go to the movies. Instead, they plowed on, understanding the value of controlling those urges. In the end, self-discipline is an investment in you.

As with many other qualities of my character, I learned self-discipline through sports. My goal always was to excel, whether it was basketball, football, or baseball, and the only way I knew how to excel was by way of a steady diet of practice. Practice meant discipline.

It wasn't enough for me to just put in the work required by my coaches; that was the minimum required for participation on the teams. My goal was to be the very best, and only a rigid schedule of extra practice could bring me my heart's desire.

As a youth, when I was not in school or doing my chores, I was honing my skills at sports. My friends would run off to do one thing or another that kids do. I would, alone, practice my game. I would visualize myself performing at a high level in a pressure-packed situation.

I would play games with myself, challenge myself, to run faster, to hit the ball more solidly, to shoot better from a particular area on the court. I was obsessed with getting better, with being the best, so no coach ever had to worry about me putting in the work. It was a part of my makeup.

This self-discipline paid off when I lettered in basketball, baseball, and football in high school. In fact, I was the all-time leading basketball scorer in Richmond High

School history, a record that lasted for more than two decades.

In fact, I held that record until it was broken by my son, Damien, who played for me at Richmond when I was coach. My self-discipline later made me a star player at George Fox University, and then a professional basketball player in Canada.

For all of my positive self-imaging and love of learning, I would never have achieved the heights I did in sports without the self-discipline to relentlessly improve, which formed an essential core of my character.

Naturally, I brought that same self-discipline to my activities as a businessman. Every little detail adds up in small business, and one hundred percent dedication is needed just to keep the venture running.

Prioritizing Priorities

Setting priorities is essential to the process of self-discipline. You have to decide what's important in your life, business and personal.

If your goal is to start a business, then you must be prepared to cast aside all distractions that stand in the way of achieving your goal. For instance, when I decided to tell part of my life story through Hollywood, I turned my businesses in Richmond over to my assistant manager and gave myself one year to achieve my goal.

The movie became the priority and so I adjusted my life accordingly.

I focused all of my energies on learning everything I could about the movie business, and I spent countless hours preparing to tell my story to the various studios. I was able to consummate a deal for the movie in considerably less time than the year I set as a goal, and I'm certain that the self-discipline I exercise played a big role in accelerating the deal. I was prepared and it came across.

My efforts included preparing a professional-looking booklet containing news articles, interviews, and pictures detailing the lockout and its aftermath. When I met with Mike Tollin, Brian Robbins, and their executive producer, Sharla Sumpter, I was able to make a complete presentation of my story, including visual aids. I did not go into the meetings just winging it.

That is the kind of self-discipline and dedication to success that I had. They took me seriously because they saw I was serious.

As the basketball coach at Richmond High, I was serious about it instilling in my players self-discipline, which was different from a positive self-image.

This was more about getting them to understand the value of committing to getting better beyond what I would do for them, not about reinforcing positive vibes.

For them, I focused on having set priorities, like winning ball games on the court and winning with good grades in the classroom. I taught that to do that meant they would have to cast aside those distractions or excuses people use to not put in the work.

On the court, this meant not cutting corners in practice. "As you practice, so goes your performance in games," I told them. It worked out so well that they began policing themselves.

If a player did not extend the required amount of effort in practice, the players gave him grief, understanding that if he would quit on them in practice, he would quit on them in a game, too.

In every practice, I required the players to run sprints the full length of the court twenty times without stopping. I would make a mental note of which players would always finish their sprints first and who was always last. When the practices started, Damien would usually finish in the middle of the pack.

But soon thereafter, Damien was consistently coming in first. He didn't achieve that just by running in practice with all of the other guys. Every morning, Damien was waking up at five o'clock to run five miles on the school track. I couldn't have been prouder of my son; he had learned the skill of self-discipline, and eventually it would lead him not only to break all of my old scoring records at the school, but also to earn a scholarship to the West Point Academy's Preparatory School.

I explained to my players that self-discipline meant focusing on the final results and not just the process. Persistence of effort will lead to consistency of results. Those kids in that neighborhood had many outside distractions that could have pulled them any number of ways: drugs, crime, gangs.

When you consider that, their self-discipline is their biggest accomplishment. It is the biggest and most important because shunning the pull from all directions to do something else allowed them to play basketball and to become quality students.

We won seven championships and they became above-average students, and it all started with them eschewing the temptation of other activities and focusing on their clear ambitions.

As much as coaches are control freaks who would like to outline and monitor how students live their lives when they are not around, it is impossible to do. It is the same with teachers and parents. There will be times when that kid is alone. What does he do then?

So, instilling self-discipline was crucial because if the students were disciplined only while in front of me or their parents or teachers, anything could have happened when they were away from us.

Our players, I'm proud to say, became model students as well as model citizens.

Imagine That

In a very real way, your imagination is the sum of your dreams. If you can't dream about attaining a certain goal, you will never reach that goal. Success is impossible without imagination.

And like positive self-image, a love of learning, and self-discipline, imagination is a skill you can learn to develop. You just have to dream big. By expanding your imagination, you will grow your chances for success in fulfilling your dreams.

Each of us has been blessed with an imagination since childhood. We've all seen the wonder on a child's face during his first encounter with all of the miracles this world has to offer.

As a child gets older, his imagination expands. The key to obtaining success as an adult is to maintain that childlike imagination.

Look at all of the famous people through history, and in most you will see that they were all dreamers before they became leaders. Leonardo da Vinci imagined the *Mona Lisa* before he ever set brush to canvas. This isn't a guess on my part—da Vinci's workshops and workbooks are filled with his drawings and plans for his paintings.

Dr. Martin Luther King, Jr., dreamed of a world where all people, black and white, despite race and creed, would live together in peace. Through this vision he helped shape the Civil Rights Movement and the dramatically better race relations we have in the United States today. Considering the times in the 1960s, Dr. King had to have a huge imagination to make that proclamation.

Dreaming is different from visualization. When you visualize, you inherently have visions of something you believe is attainable, something tangible. When you dream, there are no limitations. You stretch your visions and imagination beyond any parameters. That is how you become a true difference-maker.

I went on a promotional speaking tour in support of the opening of the movie *Coach Carter* in 2005. I visited thirty-six cities in forty days and gave inspirational speeches at each location. Amid this grind, I had engaged hundreds of people before and after my speeches.

One of those people was a man who we'll call DP for now. As we conversed, I gradually became more enthralled by DP's life story, as he told me of how he had raised his daughter on his own after his wife succumbed to cancer and other fascinating information about his journey.

I found DP's story to be inspiring, so much so that while we were talking, I imagined his tale being available to a much larger audience.

I whipped out my pad of paper and committed DP's story to writing, and later studied it at my hotel room. The next day, I placed a call to a major Hollywood producer and he agreed with me that DP's story should be made into a movie. We are currently discussing hiring a writer to capture the screenplay for the movie about DP's life story.

That's what imagination can do. It can produce big results. It takes you out of the box, out of your comfort zone, and into a place you might not have expected.

Of course, imagination also comes from deep inside all of us, although it can be inspired by the world around us. To make a dream a reality, we have to give it shape and form in the real world.

Becoming known for a movie about my life all came from my imagination, a dream. Who does that? Who dreams of their life being told via a motion picture?

Someone with imagination, that's who.

When I was just seven years old, still living in

Mississippi, my mom was cooking in the kitchen when I told her in a note: One day they will make a movie about my life. Seriously.

Where that came from, I cannot say. I did not know for what reason a film would be made about me, but I felt it enough to share with my mom, who had to say to herself, "Yeah, okay, son. Whatever you say."

To me, she said, "Okay, baby. I know they will."

Thinking back on that moment about fifty years later, I understand completely that my imagination ruled, even way back then.

When it came time for me to fulfill my imagination, I realized that while it was a big dream, it was not implausible.

So I wrote what is known as a screen treatment for my story, even though I didn't know then that that's what it was called. Then I began knocking on doors, seeking out producers and writers all over Hollywood, looking for someone to help me make my movie.

Knocking on doors got me some sore knuckles, but nothing more. Nobody seemed interested in making a movie based on my life story. But I was intent on following my imagination. I simply would not take "no" for an answer. So I stretched out my imagination further, and made up a booklet to use as a selling tool.

Relying on all of the people skills I'd learned as a small business owner and as a high school basketball coach, I began to approach these Hollywood insiders differently. I learned how to sell a story to the professionals, and then I kept knocking on doors, until finally

Paramount and MTV Films opened their doors to let me in. The rest, as they say, is history. The movie was made. My imagination was fulfilled.

All my life my imagination has run wild, and it has been a source of my successes.

When I was in high school, I dreamed one day of being the star player who won the big game with the last-second shot. I imagined the crowd roaring its approval.

In order to achieve that dream, I had to first make myself into a star player. I used my skills of self-discipline to put in the work to elevate my status from a player of potential to a player of vast achievement.

That done, my chance came. A game against our rival Kennedy High came down to the final shot. Coach Rodgers chose me, the captain, during a timeout as the player to make the final shot.

All of my hard work had paid off, by putting me in the position to realize my dream. Since I had gained acclaim as one of the best players in the country, the defense knew I would be the one taking the final shot.

But I had imagined the moment so many times that there was nothing they could do to prevent me from making the dream a rejoicing reality.

As the clock ran down, I eluded two defenders and pulled up for a jump shot. It was as if there were no noise in the building. I did not hear a thing, except for my heartbeat.

The ball left my hands softly and fell through the hoop with just one second left on the clock. That moment was not only the culmination of all of my efforts to that date, but my dream crystallizing into reality. Without an imagination, I would not have felt so comfortable in that moment.

The Spiritual Factor

Above all, I believe in a higher power other than myself. The foundation of my existence is my faith in God and His almighty power. I thank God over and over for the blessings He has bestowed upon me.

I have walked with the Lord for as long as I have walked, and my belief in Him and His Son, Jesus Christ, has helped instill in me a sense of positive self-image, a sense of imagination, and a sense that it is okay to dream big.

For me, faith in the Lord has equated to faith in myself, for how can I fail if I know that God is with me?

This is not a religious stance. This is a spiritual position. No matter which God you serve, there is a spirit of knowing where your blessings come from that should permeate your being.

In my case, it is God above whose never-ending presence in my life guides me and fuels the inner peace and positive self-worth that reside in me.

My parents saw to it that we went to church as youths, and that early start helped build in us the understanding of the power of God. There are things that happen in your life that you just cannot wholly take credit for.

The people you meet, when you meet them, the opportunities that arise...you don't know how they happen. They just do, and it is a spiritual occurrence that makes them happen.

Yes, I developed a positive self-image and persistence and an imagination and a passion for knowledge. But the foundation of God has granted me the blessings of my life.

My faith in God has been a powerful tool that I have used to build up my own sense of self-worth. Knowing God will not fail me has given me confidence to attack any challenge.

That's what spirituality is about: having faith in a higher power other than yourself. If you have trust in a higher power, you will have the capacity to trust in yourself and the world around you. As the Bible says, "Faith is the substance of things hoped for, the evidence of things not seen." If you know and understand that God has put you here for a reason, you will find the courage you need to let your imagination soar and take the actions necessary to make your dreams a reality.

From the Gospel According to Matthew, spoken by our Lord Jesus Christ in His Sermon on the Mount: "Ask, and it shall be given you; seek, and ye shall find; knock, and it shall be opened to you."

Translation: If you want success, you only have to reach out and take hold of it with both hands. Don't just try. Do.

"Seek, and ye shall find." That has been the story of my life.

At All Times, Pray

Because of my faith in the Lord, I have never been afraid to reach out and explore new vistas. I have never let my fear or doubts hold me back. When I formulate a goal, I am ready to commit myself to a new course of action one hundred percent, because I know that the Lord is with me.

Spirituality has always played an enormous role in my life. I first joined the Elk Grove Baptist Church in McComb, Mississippi, when I was a child, then I became a member of the Antioch Baptist Church in Richmond, and I have found a new church in Marlin, Texas. I am a faithful attendee on Sundays, but every day is a day of prayer for me.

No matter how high you climb in life, you can still get down on your knees and pray to the Lord for guidance. As the Bible says, "What things so ever ye desire, when ye pray, believe that ye shall receive them, and ye shall have them."

To get somewhere, you must know where you are going. But if you can't find your direction in life, then use the Lord as your compass. He won't steer you wrong. These are my fundamental strongholds on spirituality.

And here's another: "Judge not, that ye be judged. For with what judgment ye judge, ye shall be judged; and with what measure ye mete, it shall be measured to you again."

In other words, who are we to judge other people?

When I came to Hollywood, I discovered that the movie business is filled with ambitious, covetous people. Some of these people do not treat their fellow man with compassion or respect. I've run into a few of these people myself. But I've always "turned the other cheek." I stood my ground, but I never disrespect another man. Case in point: I was in a meeting with some producers, a major Hollywood actor, and a studio executive. For whatever reason, the studio executive was extremely disrespectful toward the producers and me. He only treated the major actor with respect because of his so-called "A-list" status, so he was important to a studio's success.

Now I could've returned this man's disrespect, but that is not how I was raised. I am guided by my strong sense of spirituality and I do not treat others with disrespect.

So I remained courteous and kind throughout the meeting. And even though we did not succeed in persuading this studio executive to produce our movie, the major star pulled me aside afterward and praised me for maintaining my cool.

He told me he was so impressed by my gracious manner that he wanted to work with me on getting the movie made. Having such an important star commit to the project was the surest way of getting that movie made. So here was a case where the serenity my spirituality gave me led to a positive result on my road to success.

The Bible also teaches us that charity is a quality prized above all others. I have always applied that rule to my own life. As I have gained success in Hollywood,

I have given freely of my time and energies to many young filmmakers who have sought out my help in getting into the movie business. I give of myself freely, without expectation of reward, because the giving of self is the reward.

More than once I've wound up doing business with someone I've helped along the way. Giving begets more giving. Goodness is just a part of human nature. Find the goodness in your heart, and it will spark the goodness in the hearts of others.

Picture your life as a house, using your spiritual guidance as the foundation of that house, the base upon which the whole edifice stands. And if daily accomplishments and powerful visualization form the bricks and mortar for that house, then it is faith in the Lord that bonds it all together.

God affords us the gifts of our imaginations, gives us the capacity to embrace all there is to learn, resides in us to have a positive self-image, and allows us to dream big. And so, we have limitless potential to achieve at the highest levels.

Chapter Four

R.E.S.P.E.C.T.

Aretha Franklin sang enthusiastically about respect in the 1960s, spelling out the letters in a song that was an anthem in the ideal of showing deference, regard, and admiration to others. In recent years, respect has been reduced to a kid judging how another kid looked at him as he passed by.

My players at Richmond High knew nothing of Aretha's impassioned plea for showing value and consideration of another person. When I arrived in 1999, they were caught up in the misguided association of the streets, meaning they perceived respect as something given and not earned.

As their coach, I had to change that warped mind-set. It was quite a task, as I walked into a team of players that really did not have respect for themselves, much less one another or anyone else.

I first let them know that respect was not given freely; it had to be earned. And I told them that they determined how people perceived them, how people respected them by the way they carried themselves on and especially off the court.

I created a daily exercise before practice that was the most important of the countless team-building exercises I implemented. I required each player to stand in front of his teammates and deliver a speech about anything. I wanted them to get comfortable speaking in front of people, build their confidence, while also helping them learn some things about the world.

They hated the idea.

They grumbled and complained and whined. "What does this have to do with basketball?" they said. And their parents joined in on the protest.

They didn't understand at the time that basketball was the hook, but education was the goal.

So to get them to participate, I told them that if they did not do it, they would not play in the game. What bigger discipline action was there than that?

Notice I wrote "discipline action," and not "punishment." Punishment lasts a day, a week, a month. Discipline lasts a lifetime.

They wanted nothing more than to play in the games, so they participated, if only barely.

Other than my son, Damien, who was used to public speaking at church and in school, all I got was players standing up, talking for a few minutes in a low voice, no eye contact, fidgeting, totally uncomfortable.

I let them talk about whatever they wanted, and most of them chose basketball. The next week I chose the subjects for them: classical music, art, history. So they had to know who Beethoven was and learn musical terms such as "crescendo." Then they had to do research.

They complained about that, too. I didn't care. I told them: "Our lives are a canvas. You're the ink. Now you paint your life."

I reinforced that people saw them based on what they projected. "You have to be someone who has the ability to communicate your feelings, thoughts, and energy through your actions."

We went on with the speeches every day. But while we were doing well on the court, the presentations were hardly enthusiastic. I told them, "Since you can't get that done, just leave and go to the library."

And man, did they hate leaving the court. Basketball was their identity. They were a success. We were undefeated. And I told them: "This is a part of why we're undefeated. I need you guys to know some other things besides basketball."

They didn't buy it. But then, about midseason, it was like a miracle happened. Suddenly, it kicked in. The players started enjoying the learning and became excited about speaking.

I asked for presentations one afternoon and everyone raised their hands.

I almost cried.

They had finally understood.

To that point I saw incremental progress week by

week, but nothing that would have given me an indication they had turned the corner.

But they respected the process. They started preparing for their presentations as they would prepare for games. They would practice during lunch. They would write things down. It was so exciting for me to see.

Above all, they respected themselves enough to make sure they made strong presentations. Suddenly, we started hearing these wonderful oral presentations about Mozart, the Statue of Liberty, Niagara Falls, the pyramids of Egypt, and on and on. We had one kid who was fascinated with UFOs. And then we would take it a step further by going to the library to learn more.

The turnaround was just amazing. And you could see that the respect they held for themselves took on a new meaning. They wanted to do well. And their respect extended to their teammates; they listened intently to everyone's presentations. They even paired up to do presentations together.

It was the most rewarding thing. They had stretched their minds and it changed their lives. Every day I gave them small goals I thought they could reach so they could experience what it was like to attain a goal and the satisfaction that came with it.

I had one player, Wayne, whom you could not miss. He was all muscle, a good-looking guy who was a six-foot-seven immature kid who liked telling jokes and being the class clown, which got him in trouble. He had gotten mostly F's the previous semester for playing around in class.

But he wrote phenomenal poetry and was a spoken word artist. When he opened up around midseason like his teammates, he was a great source of entertainment. You could give him a letter, say, P, and he would make up a poem using all P words. It was amazing. And he didn't have to write it down.

To this day, he gets paid to perform spoken word around the Bay Area. It was his thing and he turned those short speeches in front of his teammates into something that has gained him a measure of notoriety.

Best of all, he went from poor grades to the honor roll in one semester. You cannot tell me the respect he gained for himself was not a big part of that.

I was doing anything I could to get the players to read more. How do you get people engaged? Create competitive projects that challenge them.

Even with the oral presentations I made it competitive. At the end of the week, we voted as a team on the player who had the most interesting speech. The winner did not have to participate in the wind sprints we ran at the end of every practice.

But the great thing was that most of the winners ran the sprints anyway. They respected the team and did not want to miss out on anything. The respect they gained for one another and for themselves helped grow the team's closeness. It was a tight unit. Whatever happened within the team stayed within the team—the same way people regard a weekend in Las Vegas.

For me, it was like fifteen of my children had learned the value of earning respect in half a season. That was an emotional thing. I was totally invested in those kids—emotionally, financially, spiritually. We were a team in every sense of the word.

The Giving of Self

When I graduated from college, I had my whole life planned out. I had an offer to play professional basketball in Canada, which could have opened up an opportunity to play in the National Basketball Association. But my life was about to take a sudden turn. My girlfriend was pregnant with our child.

At first, I thought it was enough for me to make visits between games to see my son, Damien, and to send him money from the road. But my father, whom I respect and trust so much, called me and told me that my first duty was to my son, that I had a responsibility to see that my son was raised up the right way, and that he had a loving, caring home where I could nurture his body and his spirit.

It was not a hard decision. I wanted my son to respect and honor me. That was extremely important to me.

So I gave up my dreams of playing in the NBA and came home to take care of my son. I did not hesitate to give up my aspirations, but it was not an easy thing to do. What kid with any amount of talent does not want to be a pro ballplayer? I wasn't any different. But growing up the way I did made me more mature than most. And I respected my father so much that his words overpowered any lingering thoughts I had of trying to make the NBA.

So for the next sixteen years, I became Damien's primary caretaker. His mother agreed that a boy being raised by a man was the best option at that time. It was not an easy decision for her. But she, like me, believed I could help guide his life from a male's perspective on a day-to-day basis. So she let me do my parental job.

I changed his diapers, fed him when he was hungry, cared for him when he was sick, and watched over him while he slept. In order to provide a loving home for him, I enlisted the aid of my mother and seven sisters. To provide us both with a means of support, I resurrected my old dreams and started a sporting goods store, running my own business so I could plan my schedule around the needs of my son. And I took every bit of knowledge and wisdom that I had learned from my own parents and passed them on to Damien. Of course, I taught him to play basketball from the first day he could walk.

In raising my son, I learned the true meaning of giving to others. Not once did I think of myself when I gave myself over to parenthood. But Damien has blessed me with so many rewards I cannot even begin to count or measure them. What price can you place on a father's pride when he sees his son take his first step, make his first basket, or achieve his first A in school?

How can anyone place a value on a man seeing his son develop the self-discipline and imagination to achieve his own lofty goals in life? When Damien graduated from high school and received a scholarship to

West Point, I felt that I had gained a greater reward than any other success I had achieved in my life.

And just as important is having the respect of my son. I earned it in raising him. That's what comes with giving and sacrificing—respect.

If you put more time in at work, come early and stay late, you earn the respect of your managers and peers. If you sacrifice a weekend trip to prepare for an important Monday morning meeting, you earn respect.

Dressed for Success

Just as it was projected in the movie, when I walked into the gym for the first time as coach of Richmond High, I was dressed in a suit and tie. And some of the players laughed. Others took it as a sign that I thought I was better than they were. Still others did not know what to think.

What they ended up learning was that a suit and tie was my work attire. Other than when I would change to sometimes participate in practice on the court—demonstrate exactly how a drill should be run or how a player should move or position himself—I was in a suit and tie. Every single day, without exception, that's what I wore.

I wore it for effect, but not to impress. I always believed it was really important to be professional in all things I did. The way I dressed was part of my presentation to the world. I was dressing for success. I was trying to live a life of excellence.

In a suit and tie, I was never overdressed. I could go into a formal meeting when that was required. But if there was another scenario I was involved in where a suit was too much, I could take off the jacket and tie and be appropriate. Or I could loosen the tie in relaxed situations and keep it moving.

But when you are underdressed, you cannot make the kind of adjustments I am able to make on the spot. It would require you either to bring more clothes or to go home and get more clothes, which means you could lose the moment.

Of course, people see you in a suit and intuitively offer a measure of respect. A suit means you are ready to do business.

So, like all my challenges with my players, demanding in their contract with me that they wear a white shirt and tie on game days was something not greeted with much excitement.

It was the opposite of cool. They were used to the attire of the day, which usually meant baggy jeans hanging way too low, oversized shirts, and sneakers. I was not going to accept that.

I told them that first day, "The losing stops today. It's about winning out there, in everyday life."

They could not win in life if they did not know the proper way to dress outside of their school clothes. Just as with the oral presentations, the parents complained. Many of the kids did not have anything other than what they wore to school and their parents could not afford to purchase new outfits.

So I told them to go to the Goodwill or thrift store, where the items required were no more than a few dollars each. The complaining continued, but I was not going to bend.

Of course, everyone conformed. And as we grew into a tightly knit team that won a lot and respected and enjoyed one another's company, the issue of attire faded like dust in the wind.

Wearing a shirt and tie added to their stature as big shots at school. They stood out for something positive, something great. The community rallied around the team, and they looked like the respectable men they grew into.

That was another goal achieved. I have been asked a lot about how difficult it was to get the kids' respect. But it was not difficult. Kids are perceptive. I think, after the natural initial doubting, they knew I cared a great deal about them. They figured it out from day one, but I had to confirm it for them over time.

People don't care about how much you know until they figure out how much you care. With them knowing I cared, I was able to blaze new trails and endeavors with them.

I think it helped that I never tried to overimpress them. I treated them as young adults. I conducted myself as a man. I think they respected right away the way I spoke to them.

I was not a yeller as a coach. I just don't think that works very well, especially with getting and sustaining the attention of the people you manage. Now, did I yell?

Yes. As a coach and leader, there come points when you have to be more demonstrative than others. But it was not a consistent part of my leadership makeup.

You scream and yell all the time and at some point it becomes garbled noise. Your players don't hear it anymore. Or at the very least, it does not have any impact. But if you raise your voice at choice moments, moments that call for urgency, you will get their attention every time because they become conditioned that yelling by Coach means something really important.

The Goal of Goals

The best way to have a stagnant organization is to let those on your team just go for it with no real destination in mind. Without a road map, most would go aimlessly about their job, uninspired to get beyond a certain point.

Rather, most people need a defined goal to strive for to give them purpose and tangible evidence of success.

I like to think in terms of the three H's. Head. Heart. Hands.

A goal starts in the head. That is where everything originates, where intellectual ambitions—big and small—come together.

It then travels to the heart. That is where the goal becomes coveted and something you care about reaching. It is nurtured and takes the form of something special.

And then it moves to the hands. That is where the work gets done. The labor. The execution. The payoff.

A lot of people think you simply put an exercise DVD in the player and you will lose weight. No! It actually takes some effort. You have to do some work. You really must break a sweat if you want to shed pounds.

I told my team: Winning in life is working toward a worthwhile goal. And so they wanted to know what the goals should be. In their lives, they did not know the value of dreaming big—beyond the ever-common making-it-to-the-pros dream.

They did not have the resources or know anyone with the resources. So they had to do it themselves. And the things we really want to do in life, we get them done. If we really, really want it, we figure out a way to get it.

I had to make them understand that. I knew if I could slowly change their way of thinking, get them to act on good thoughts, they would be able to change their lives. Not me. They would do it.

So it was important for them to know that a worthwhile goal did not mean they had to end up rich and famous. It could mean being a strong provider for your family or planting a garden. It did not mean you needed a large bank account to be happy. It could mean you were respected in the community because you were honorable and hardworking, the way firemen and police officers are.

There are endless meaningful goals in the world. The operative word being "meaningful."

My players had a rough upbringing. Richmond, California, was and remains a tough town plagued by crime and drugs and substandard services, including and especially schools. But the purpose of taking them to the homeless shelter was twofold: to inspire them to volunteer to help there and to let them see that as bad as they thought they had it, there were others in more dire conditions.

They left thinking, "I could be here." They then had the inspiration not to end up in a shelter. They had a meaningful goal.

That is the goal of goals: To inspire ambition.

People talk themselves out of success all the time. But you have to become your own GPS system. If you do A, B, C, it should get you to D—if you established a meaningful goal.

On top of all that, once you reach your goal, your self-respect rises and so does the respect of your peers toward you.

That self-respect manifested itself in my players in how they achieved in the classroom. Simply, every player I ever coached graduated from Richmond High.

The idea always has been education over basketball, and to see those young men proudly get their diplomas year after year was rewarding. The way they walked across the stage was significant. Their heads were up. They were proud.

It was a totally different posture from when I first encountered them. But they had accomplished something they were proud of and earned the respect of their teachers and classmates.

Coach Carter Carrot

I used to name some of our plays after my seven sisters. And on occasion, I would name plays after my players' family members. One game, Courtney, our six-foot-eight center, was playing awful. I took him out for a few minutes and he went back in and he actually played worse. At halftime I asked him what was wrong. He said, "Coach, you wouldn't understand." His girlfriend was upset with him and he just could not play. So at halftime I drew up a play called Stephanie, his girlfriend's name. He took the ball out right where she was sitting at half-court with her friends. Slapped the ball and called out, "Stephanie." We ran a backdoor play and got a dunk. Stephanie's girlfriend, who was sitting next to her, started to scream, "They have a play named after you." Courtney played well after that. And when the game was over, he said, "Coach, you saved my life." Courtney had fallen back into the good graces of his girlfriend because of that play, so he was able to relax after that and play up to his standards.

It's What You Say and How You Say It

Not only was I not a yeller, but I also afforded most everyone I confronted with deference.

I often started or ended a conversation with "young man." It was another reason I had the respect of my team.

But it was and still is a part of my personality. It is a form of giving respect. You say, "Yes sir" or "no ma'am" or "young lady" or "young man," and you instantly are giving someone respect. And that empowers people.

I am quick to point out if someone looks good by giving a compliment. It is sincere and it puts people at ease, makes them look at you in a particular way. It is a form of earning respect.

It all started at home with my family. My dad had a second-grade education. But he had a depth of wisdom gained from life experiences and innate smarts.

He was well liked in the community. He had a farm and he employed people and earned respect just by who he was. He was not very loquacious. He was hardworking and all about providing for his family.

My mom had a sixth-grade education. She was a committed worker, too. But she's my mom. Your mother is your first teacher because she carries you through the pregnancy and then spends probably ninety-five percent of her time with you after birth.

The respect she and my dad received from her children was natural. We did not talk about respect at all growing up. It was just there. A bird doesn't have to be taught how to build a nest. A spider spins a web naturally. Some things are just innately given to us. That's how respect for parents is.

From watching my parents and sisters and brother, I learned about how to comport myself in a way that would earn respect. We're a close family. With my brother and sisters, we're still our own best friends.

The other influence I had in my life was my high school basketball coach, Mr. Roy Rogers. It was under his tutelage that I blossomed into Richmond High's all-time leader in scoring, assists, and steals.

But as meaningful and fun as it was to be that successful, Coach Roger's influence as a leader was even more important. He took a lot of time with me. I used to see him play semipro basketball. He conducted himself in a certain manner, dressed a certain way. He had a great choice of words. He did not raise his voice and he always seemed to be thinking.

He did not ask for respect. He demanded your respect in a very good way. It was Coach Rogers who asked me to take over for him as coach at my alma mater.

I did so because he asked me—that's how much I respect him as a man. He believed I could help the young men and that helped me believe I could do it.

Still, I did not know the enormity of the job. We had some bad days at Richmond High, which was good. Sometimes you need a little rain to appreciate the sunny days. The good news is that we had a lot of sun shine on us. Spring always follows winter. And there's a reason for that—it gives us a new start.

Quotable

In my experiences of leadership, I have come up with many little phrases and ideals that hold big meanings around respect and honor and success:

- When you have success in one walk of life, you can see yourself successful in other walks of life. Your confidence stretches and you are bound by nothing.
- Successful people make one good decision after another, after another. And when they make a mistake, they are able to pull from all those wins to keep pressing forward.
- The best five words you can ever say to a person is: "You did a good job." Those kinds of statements earn you respect. They go a long way with the receiver and help in building confidence.
- When I hear people give up by saying, "I did everything I could," I think, "Really? Well, did you go look for the kid when he cut class? Did you go to his home? Did you go talk to both parents, who live in different locations?" Well, I did all that. There is no reason to ever give up.
- Good thinkers will always be in demand. Knowing how to do the job will keep you in the job. Knowing why will keep you as boss. That's why being a good thinker solves problems and builds great organizations. With my team, there were times when we got where we thought we couldn't lose a game. We were thinking success and it carried over to how we performed at key moments of close games.
- People do business with people they like. When you are well liked, when you are kind and generous to people, people respond to that. And those

traits show up in your work. And when your work speaks for itself, don't interrupt.

- Ninety-five percent of the people in the world are kind and generous. It's just that we somehow find the five percent who are not. But that should never deter us from being who we are supposed to be: kind and generous.
- When you're successful, you see obstacles, not problems.
- Coach Carter Law: I don't accept any excuses because I don't make any. When I don't know something, I can say with a lot of confidence, "I just don't know." And then I go searching. Ask, knock, search. There are tools to get the answers, and I get them.

People respect that.

Chapter Five

Cultivating a Family Atmosphere

At age nineteen, my big sister Diane moved from rural Mississippi to Northern California. I was only six. It was a significant occasion for our family in a number of ways.

First of all, my mom was bold enough to say, "I'm sending my baby out there into the world."

That was big because Diane—we called her "Ann"—had no exposure beyond the country town of McComb, which is the same as saying she had no exposure at all. That world out there was especially big to her.

Ann did not necessarily want to go, but my mom understood the value of her getting someplace where she could stretch the boundaries of her imagination. Even though she had just graduated from high school, she already had hit the walls of growth in Mississippi—unless, of course, she wanted to do domestic work.

99

When I look back upon what Ann did—leaving home fresh out of high school and moving to the West—I'm still impressed. What a tremendous amount of courage, confidence, and discipline that took.

My mom saw something much bigger for her—for all of us—and sent Ann on her way. When it was time for her to pack and go, the entire family stood there and cried. My big sister was leaving home, the first of the nine kids to go. It was devastating. Recalling it now brings tears to my eyes.

Ann was the leader among the team of kids. She was, in essence, the second mother. But Momma decided it was time for her to go. Kids leave home every day for college. This was something different. This was leaving to go start your own life, at eighteen years old.

And here's the thing: We virtually had no money. There was twenty-five dollars in the entire family. That was it. I knew how much because my parents were very transparent. The money was kept in a jar in the kitchen.

But my momma gave Ann twenty for the trip, leaving the family with five dollars. There was no way she could travel and leave us at home with such a small amount of money. So a family friend we called Aunt Polly rode out there with her to California.

That was some impressive leadership by my mother. Sometimes, as a leader or manager, you have to assess those under you and determine when or how much more responsibility they deserve and can handle. My mom determined that Ann was enough of a leader in her own right to go across country and make a life for herself, based on her role as pretty much the second mom. She ran the house when my parents were out working.

And my mom was right. Ann found her way. We kept the jar in the kitchen and would put money in there—a penny here, a nickel there—to send out to her as she worked to get on her feet.

It was not too long before she enrolled in community college and secured a job in a hospital as a lab technician. She has held a job with that same hospital, moving up the ranks, for the last forty-five years.

By the time we got somewhat comfortable with Ann's absence, the next sister, Ernestine, was prepared to move on. Her destination: Indiana.

COACH CARTER CARROT

When my sister Diane moved to California at eighteen, she worked hard to get established. But she always had her heart at home and on her younger sisters and brothers. For instance, she would send my youngest sister, Deborah, a dollar bill cut in half on a Monday. On Wednesday, I would get in the mail the other half of the dollar. So, we had to work together to make the dollar whole. Deborah would want a nickel more than the fifty cents she was entitled to, so we had to negotiate and compromise at a very young age to settle the one-dollar debate. She was teaching us to work together and to compromise.

She had the same work ethic and job loyalty as Ann. She stayed on her job for twenty years.

Ernestine had three kids, who all went on to college. And she has grandkids who are college graduates. But growing up, what I remember most about her was she was a fighter.

She was like my grandmother on my mother's side: tough. She would fight on a moment's notice. She even would fight our brother. She didn't care. There was no fear in her. In that way, she was the strength of the family, the enforcer.

Barbara was the next to leave the Mississippi farm. Her destination: Chicago with her new husband, who took a job there.

We called Barbara "Cookie." She was Miss Personality. Very outgoing and fun-loving. People gravitated to her because she was so pleasant.

And she could sing so beautifully, the voice of an angel. At the same time, she was very bold. She would say what needed to be said and would try anything. She was defiant.

She would be told something she could not do, but she would do it anyway and say, "I'll just take the punishment."

Then there was Hattie Jean. She was small and looked just like my mother. She was the philosopher, the peacemaker. Hattie Jean would encourage you not to argue with your siblings and to eat your vegetables—that kind of thing. She just wanted everything to be right and for everyone to do right.

And she was an excellent student. She took great pride in her grades and studied long and hard to make sure her report card reflected her commitment.

After her was Mary, whom we called Grace. She suffered from epilepsy, and even though she was on medication, she would have seizures at any time.

She could be talking to you one minute and on the ground the next. But she was as strong a person as anyone else you could find. Because the seizures were so random, she would fall and break an arm or a leg. But she'd get a cast put on it and was back to smiling. Amazing.

Nothing could break her spirit. Epilepsy did not prevent her from being happy—or a great student who went on to college.

Also, Grace taught me how to write. We could not afford paper, so she would write in the sand and give me exercises to improve my penmanship. When people now compliment me on my writing or penmanship, I immediately think of Grace. It was her doing. She's just kind and generous.

After her came Linda, who was very athletic. At pickup basketball games, she would get drafted before most boys. That's how good she was.

She was also a fantastic musician. She played the clarinet and taught me how to as well, though I ended up switching to the saxophone.

Linda was just very talented. She graduated from the University of Southern California, got her master's degree, and had two children, who also are college graduates.

The baby sister was Deborah, who followed the education path laid before her and graduated from college and earned a master's degree, too. She has been an entrepreneur all her life, even as she worked for twenty-five years at PacBell.

My brother, Junior, was a role model for me. I stuck my little chest out when I was a kid, telling people I was Albert Carter Jr.'s brother. He was an amazing athlete, an All-American in football.

He was so good that he gave our family status. We were known around our little town because he was a dominant athlete. I learned about commitment from Junior. He would go to bed by nine o'clock at night to get his rest and do his push-ups and whatever else he had to do to stay in shape.

Those are my siblings, my team. We all were totally different in how we acted, thought, looked, dealt with people...just about everything. But we formed a bond that was unbreakable and we learned from each other.

In fact, our differences helped us blossom into a finely tuned unit that worked well together.

Growing Together at Home and at Work

There is not a time in my life when I do not remember working. With a farm in rural Mississippi, there was plenty of work to go around. We all—girls included—put in long hours on that farm.

That's what my parents believed in: getting the job

done. Working gave us a sense of responsibility, which bred the work ethic and teamwork. These are the same elements needed to function in business.

You cannot choose your family, but you can, in the workplace, build teams full of talented individuals who complement one another.

That's why my brother and sisters and I operated so well together—we all brought something different into the equation to make the whole better.

Better yet, even though we grappled with one another as family members will do, when it was time to get a job done, we knew how to rally together to accomplish the deed.

It helped that at different points we had leaders who were intent on sharing their knowledge for the good of those under them. That's what a manager has to do— spread his wealth of expertise to others to build a cohesive unit.

Ann was our first leader, a notch below our mother. She cooked and cleaned and dished out assignments to us to get the house in order—and to make sure we stayed on task with our schoolwork. Whatever the case, Ann had it covered.

She passed down that same diligence to her younger sisters and brothers. We became a strong team around the house and the farm because—even with our various personality traits—we had someone at the helm whose own work ethic and commitment were so strong and evident. It inspired us to be similarly diligent.

Ann really instilled in us the ability to go beyond the

call of duty to make things happen. That's why she sent Deborah and me half of a dollar bill. She was way out in California, had left the nest, but still was sending us exercises on how to get along together, how to work together—an element that too often is overlooked in business.

Through Deborah, I learned about negotiations because of that split dollar bill. I always ended up getting something less than the fifty cents entitled to me because she bargained her way to an extra nickel.

I put that negotiation skill set to use when my older sisters used to date. When I was six or seven, they would have their boyfriends on the front porch and I would be right there with them. They would always want to get rid of me.

So, I would go, but only after the boy chopped the wood that was there for me to chop as early as five in the morning. That was the price for getting me to give them some privacy.

Inevitably, they did it. They did not want to get all sweaty chopping wood, but I made it so that was the only way they would be able to get rid of me. And it worked.

I carried those negotiation skills with me—all the way to Hollywood, where there was so much back-and-forth about the movie *Coach Carter*. Standing my ground when I was a kid set me up to stand my ground as a man in Hollywood—and I got what I sought there and in most cases.

The Education of Life

All of what my brother and sisters and I achieved and grew into is a testament to my parents. They were the CEOs of the family. They gave us a path to walk. They were firm in raising and disciplining us, but they were fair. At the time, I thought they were unfair.

But you know what? The older I get, the smarter my parents get.

My dad, who has since passed, was called A. J. by most everyone, although his given name was Albert. It's amazing he was schooled to only the second grade. He was a smart and wise man who was able to pick up on knowledge through observing and talking to people.

For the longest time, I didn't know he couldn't read. Though he could not read a book, he could read the blueprints to a house, something I couldn't do. He was quite an individual.

He had to drop out of school after the second grade to help support his family. There was no other option. There were twelve in his family and he had to chip in, even as a kid.

He did what he had to do and he grew into an honorable man. He believed in working and taking care of his family. That's all he saw from his dad.

I raised just one child, and I know all that came with that. He provided for nine kids and a wife. I know there were days when he didn't feel like going to work, but he *had* to go. He was persistent at what he did. He was a perfectionist.

Not only did he do tedious work, but it was very strenuous work. He worked very hard doing laborious jobs such as cutting down trees, jobs that required a lot of recovery time. But he didn't have much time to recover. He just pressed on.

In fact, he would come home after about ten hours of basically working like a slave for someone else and then he would put in another hour or two on our farm.

Our farm was everything to us. We got every meal from there. We planted and nurtured all our crops. There were greens, cucumbers, peas, cabbage, potatoes, beans, watermelons, and just about anything you can think of. You couldn't get it any fresher than what we had on that farm. It was about the size of two football fields, which tells you how much ground we had to cover.

But here's the thing: My dad pulled himself out of bed every morning at five. I would lie there tired and sleep, but I could hear him putting wood in the stove to heat up the house, if it was winter.

About an hour later, we would get up and get started working before we went to school. We also had animals on the farm—hogs, cows, horses, chickens—and they had to be fed and watered. That was among my before-the-sun-came-up jobs.

I wasn't happy about having to work so early in the morning, but who was I to complain? My father did a hundred times more work and he never complained. He just did what he had to do as an honorable man. And that says a lot about him.

I had a great role model in him. I know my work ethic and penchant for hard work and dedication allowed me to finish high school and college and travel the world—all the things he didn't do.

It was the same with my mom, Hettie, who made it to sixth grade before having to quit and help support her family. She, too, worked all her life and learned through living and raising us. That's an education that you cannot put a price tag on.

My mom worked in cahoots with my dad. He did his job to tend to the crops. Mother's job was to prepare the food and to preserve it, can it to eat later.

And I believe wholeheartedly that's why all of my sisters and brother and I are in good health—we know how to eat well because we were self-sufficient with our farm. There was no going out to restaurants. Every meal was prepared from what we produced.

My mother was a domestic who took great pride in her work. She took great pride in everything she did, a trait that seeped down to her children.

Just as important was her leadership around the house. My father was no-nonsense. My mom negotiated the arguments between the kids and—and here's the big part—she kept the house organized. The house had order. The family was organized, in how we worked around the house, on the farm... in everything.

We had to be with so many kids. Everyone knew their

place and we played our roles. It was very much like a team, which is what family is, actually.

That is not to say it was all smooth sailing. It wasn't. There was never an abundance of anything—just enough to survive. And there was adversity. There were years when winter came early and the crops died. But my dad would always know what to do and how to do it. He was always proactive in addressing problems or potential problems.

We lived a lot on poverty emotions: desire, faith, love, enthusiasm, hope. They carried us through, as it was quite a task to raise nine kids, especially when money was so hard to come by. They worked a limited budget better than anyone could imagine. That lets you know that in a business environment, with some real thought and ingenuity, so much can be accomplished.

They did not have much of a formal education, but they understood that the biggest difference to getting something and not getting something is an education, which explains why we all went on to college. They made sure we had access to more than they did.

When you have parents like that directing your upbringing, the chances for success are greater. It's like planting a garden. If you plant good seeds, you get good crops.

You can't put good seeds in bad soil and expect them to grow. There would be no nutrients. At the same time, you can't plant bad seeds in good soil. They have to work together.

My parents were the good soil and we were the good

seeds. Their organization bred togetherness. In families and in a business office, the biggest misunderstanding is that of entitlement.

Everything you get, you should deserve because you earned it. That's how it works: You deserve something only after you put in the work. And that's how it was in our household. And that's how it should be in the office, too. You are entitled only to an opportunity—that's what America affords. Beyond that, it is up to you to put in the effort, commitment, and knowledge to get where you desire.

Going the Distance

When I coached at Richmond High, my gym was the office. We ran things as a business, but as a family business.

I showed my players how important they were to me by extending myself with my efforts, my time, my finances. It was all for the greater good of them becoming better, more well-rounded people and athletes.

I showed them how much my family meant to me by naming plays after my sisters. I paid homage to them that way. Diane was a full-court press. Ernestine was a pass-and-cut offense, and on and on.

And as I mentioned before, I named some plays after my players' parents, family members, girlfriends. Anything to make them connected to the cause and to see the value of family.

I didn't understand the enormity of the job when I took it. I looked at it as my alma mater and that I could go in and make a difference.

Turned out that it brought me closer to my family because I was building a family within my team. And all the things we did way back in Mississippi—working together, challenging each other, rewarding each other—were nuggets of my life that I could share with my job.

And here's a wonderful thing about coaching at Richmond High: It made me a better coach, a better person, a better father, a better son, a better brother.

The Courage of Children

One of the great things about being a kid is that you are fearless. It's when we become adults that we lose courage.

As a kid in Mississippi, I used to swim in a watering hole near the family farm. My friends and I would congregate there almost every day. But there was one area of the watering hole that I avoided at all costs, a high cliff that stood about twenty feet over the water. Whenever I approached that cliff, I would look over the side and a sense of terror would seize me as I looked down into the depths of the water far below me.

Some of my friends weren't afraid to make that leap from the cliff into the water, and they used to tease me because of my fear of heights. I became angry because I lacked the courage of my friends, and I made it my goal to conquer my fear. There was no other way to take on the challenge except to make the leap from that cliff.

My first effort took me nearly an hour. Whenever I peered over the edge, I found myself paralyzed with terror. Finally I forced myself to jump. I seemed to fall forever through the air. But when the cool water closed over me, I knew that I had done it. I had conquered my fear.

I climbed right back up to the top of that cliff and made the leap again. Before the day was done, I had put my doubts and fears behind me completely and was jumping off the cliff with utter abandon.

I learned way back then that to beat your fears, you must confront them. They will not go away if you don't.

As confident as I was about doing the job at Richmond High, there remained a certain amount of fear in what I had in front of me. Interjecting my life into the job—my brothers and sisters and life experiences—personalized it for me. It made it familiar and warm. It made that cliff easier to jump off.

What it comes down to is this: The life lessons learned growing up could help cultivate a feeling of family in the workplace. When there is a family or team-like environment, how could that hurt?

It all comes back to leadership. A leader is courageous, even in the face of personal, emotional decisions. Momma was not looking to get rid of Ann when she was a teenager. It hurt her so much to send her daughter out into the world. And it was scary at first. But in the end, it was the best thing to do.

My mom and dad found the courage, confidence, and discipline to improve their lives, and it works the same with young people today. Confidence comes with confronting one's fears, not running from them.

Chapter Six

Persistence Makes Perfect... Or Close to It

When I was seven years old, I came home from school feeling happy-go-lucky, only to find my mom in the kitchen crying. I felt so bad and helpless.

She was concerned about being unable to provide food: She had eleven mouths to feed and not enough oil to cook beyond the meal she was preparing. That's how it was for us. We were a hardworking family that could save a little for a rainy day—but the rainy days came too often.

With my mother in distress, I used the only weapon in my arsenal at that time—pencil and paper. And I wrote her a note in cursive.

It said, "One day they are going to make a movie about me."

I had no idea where it came from, but I believed it. I remember that. What I was trying to say was that one day I would be successful enough to take care of her and she would not have to cry over finances.

To feel that at that age was not a prodigious thing. It was a kid's ambition based on a kid's experiences. Simply put, I thought the only people who were successful were people you saw on television.

On TV, I saw Marilyn Monroe, Elvis, Diana Ross, Billy Dee Williams, and Lucille Ball. They were on TV so that meant they had to be doing something right. I did not know success came in so many other forms. The mind of a seven-year-old.

My mom just hugged me. She said, "Oh, my baby…" in a way that indicated she was comforted in knowing that I cared. But I made her laugh, thereby lifting her spirits.

And unbelievably, thirty-five years later, there actually was a movie made about me and my life—well, at least part of my life. My mom and I laugh about that now.

But the reality was that I planted a seed that I spent my entire life nurturing. I learned from that experience that your ambitions always have to be somewhat unrealistic. You have to see yourself in places and then act like you belong there.

My goal in life, from the moment I made that bold, unsuspecting declaration, was to be successful, to make my mother proud, to keep her from worrying about bills.

To accomplish it required so much, but above all persistence. I would not be deterred.

Disabling the Disability

Not even a learning disability I did not know I had until I was in college prevented me from getting where I wanted to go.

It was not until then that I was diagnosed with dyslexia, an inherited condition that makes it difficult to read, write, and spell in your native language—despite at least average intelligence. And it often results in transposing letters, words, and numbers.

One of my professors noticed one day that I would invert letters or words. Before long, doctors were telling me I was dyslexic. I had never even heard the word. I didn't know what it meant. I was thinking it was a rash on my hand. I was just totally ignorant as to what it was.

But me being me, once I was diagnosed, I immediately filled my mind with research to learn more about dyslexia. I learned that dyslexia results from a neurological difference, meaning a brain difference. People with dyslexia have a larger right hemisphere in their brains than those of normal readers. It is believed that is one reason people with dyslexia often have significant strengths in areas controlled by the right side of the brain, such as artistic, athletic, and mechanical gifts. In some cases, dyslexic people even have 3-D visualization ability, outstanding musical talent, creative problem solving skills, and intuitive people skills.

Other than seeing in 3-D and outstanding musical talent, all those "symptoms" fit me to a T.

117

In addition to unique brain structure, people with dyslexia have what they call "unusual wiring." Neurons are found in unusual places in the brain, and are not as neatly ordered as in nondyslexic brains.

On top of that, MRI studies have shown that people with dyslexia do not use the same part of their brain when reading as other people. Regular readers consistently use the same part of their brain when they read. People with dyslexia do not use that part of their brain, and there appears to be no consistent part used among dyslexic readers.

So, it is assumed that people with dyslexia are not using the most efficient part of their brain when they read. A different part of their brain has taken over that function.

Once I was made aware of it, it all made sense to me. I would read something once and not get it. A second time would be clearer. A third time would almost make sense. And then that fourth time I would get it. It was how I always was. But I never thought anything of it. I thought that's how everyone read. Something that would take another person four minutes to read and comprehend would take me fifteen minutes.

For me now, to this day, it's about concentration and paying attention to small details. I go over stuff several times to make sure I understand. I used the term "learning disability" earlier, which does not mean an inability to learn.

It means learning can be more difficult in the case of people with dyslexia, not impossible. I looked it up through the National Institutes of Health, which said: "The term 'learning disability' means a disorder in one or more of the basic processes involved in understanding spoken or written language. It may show up as a problem in listening, thinking, speaking, reading, writing, or spelling or in a person's ability to do math, despite at least average intelligence."

There is no medicine that can reverse the condition. Counseling or therapy does not work. It is really about educating yourself and having a true persistence about overcoming it.

Learning about my dyslexia made me even more determined to succeed. It was the perfect opportunity for me to fall back and either feel sorry for myself or become less committed to fulfilling my ambitions.

All I knew was I had to get it done, whatever the task. I have learned that persistence is a stronger force than failure.

It goes back to being fed up with being broke as a kid—not having enough was an enlightening place for me. I knew I had to work and be better than the next guy. If I wanted to have all the comforts of life and to help my mother, I had to work harder for them. Learning I had dyslexia reinforced the drive in me that already existed.

If an opportunity arose, I would give my best effort, whether or not I liked doing the job or chore.

Thinking about it, after the initial shock of the diagnosis, I became almost obsessed with overcoming it. The competitor in me came out. I battled the disorder as

I would take on defenders when I was an All-American high school basketball player.

Dyslexia mostly impacts your ability to read, so I read more than ever after learning I had it. I consumed books at a rate most book club members did not even approach.

Every day I read as much as possible, which speaks to my desire to learn but also my persistence in not letting dyslexia believe for a second that it has a chance to beat me.

The other area in which dyslexia hampers you is writing. Well, I write all the time, from books to speeches to daily journals to my goals for the next day—and anything that comes up in between.

No doubt, I write so much because I believe in the power of seeing things on paper. But there remains this persistent notion not to be held back by dyslexia. And the way to prove that to me is to write (and read) as much as possible.

The Confidence Factor

Being persistent builds character and confidence. I would not wish dyslexia on anyone. It is no joke. But knowing I am dyslexic has inspired me to be even more persistent than I was, and that persistence has boosted my confidence into the stratosphere.

How? Being persistent meant that I worked harder

than everyone. I put in more time, more effort. I was driven. I did not rely on raw talent and I did not ever get complacent. I always strove to be better.

And the way to build confidence is strictly through preparation. Michael Jordan exuded confidence on the basketball court not only because he was extremely gifted as an athlete. That certainly helped. But it was all the work he put in that fed his confidence to where he believed in his ability to get it done. He was the best player because he had the most talent and he worked the hardest.

Talent and persistence get you a lot of places.

Your position has to be: How can I get around this problem, over it, under it...to the other side? The more planning you do, the better chance you have of defeating that problem. Planning requires considering any condition that may arise. People say practice makes perfect? No, practice makes you better.

Everyone is always in search of perfection. It is not attainable. But you can be a hard worker who plans, which helps build confidence to achieve the mission.

With my Richmond High team, I had to build confidence through first being persistent with them about what we were going to achieve. I equated my team to my family life in many instances. Even though we had so many rough times when I grew up, I always knew we would survive.

With my team, I always knew we would win. There

was talent there, it was a functional dysfunctional team, so to speak. I had to build on their commitment to be persistent, meaning not to quit, but to push on through adversity.

They were used to doing things one way, which was not necessarily the right way. So many times you see young people who believe talent alone will be enough to get them where they want to get. And then when a roadblock appears, they succumb.

I built my team's morale and self-esteem, as related in earlier chapters, through outside interests and challenges. I also worked hard at building a resistance in them to withstand the challenges they would face not only on the court, but also in the classroom and in life.

By putting parameters on them, I was able to harness the players' penchant to go left when others were going right. They started to win on the court and in the classroom, making it easier for me to reaffirm the notion of being persistent when trouble showed up.

Pretty soon, they came to believe they would win every game, no matter whom we faced or how big the deficit we had to overcome. Being persistent became a way of life, and it really manifested itself in how they chose to elevate their grades after I locked the gym because many had not met the academic requirements.

Suddenly, kids who were struggling at home, in school, and in basketball were confident about how they could function in all three areas of their lives. That persistence to achieve grew in them to where they believed in themselves—in all aspects of life.

COACH CARTER CARROT

One of my players at Richmond High was a struggling student, getting mostly C's and D's. But as he managed to meet each daily requirement for learning as set down by me and his teachers, his confidence and determination to learn more expanded. When he got the first B of his life, he wanted to achieve all B's. But when he got his first A, he was never satisfied with a B again. In just two years, this athlete blossomed into a B-plus student who earned a full academic scholarship to UC-Berkeley as an English major. That's what success can do—it can make you want more for yourself.

Don't Look Back

One of the chief problems associated with lack of success is the inability to put the past where it is—in the past. Some people just cannot let go, and even as they flounder in events of the past, they focus on where they have been instead of where they want to go.

Bad move.

Try running across a field while looking back—you will not go fast and you likely could run into something. But if you run across a field looking straight ahead, not only will you see where you're going, but you will get there much faster.

That's how it is with life and business. Mistakes happen. Unfortunate situations occur. To get past those scenarios requires the mind-set of a French race car driver.

The high-powered car he maneuvers around the track does not have a rearview window, as if to say what goes on behind me has no bearing on where I'm headed.

It is hardly that easy to do in life, but it is required if one is to truly make headway in his own life or business.

Using my players as an example, almost ninety percent of them came from an impoverished background where there was a single parent raising them, and resources and exposure outside Richmond were extremely limited.

I made it so that when they arrived in the gym for games or practices, their other world was someplace unreachable. They could not succeed if they were worrying about the turmoil outside the gym or the classroom.

That's why I took them away from the school on short trips—not only so they could see the possibilities, but also so they could mentally move themselves further and further from their current plight.

At the same time, I stressed that there is value in having unfortunate experiences in the past. From all situations, we can learn. So the idea should be to recall the troubles to learn from them, but leave them where they are—in the past.

The Right Attitude Saves the Day

How you view life is all about attitude. If you view it head on, you have a better chance to push forward. The road to success is always under construction. Sometimes the path is not so well lit. But you still have to navigate your way through it.

When your attitude is right—when you have, as I like to call it, a PMA, or positive mental attitude—there are no limitations. Your attitude tells you every day what to expect out of your life.

Every situation will not be tailor-made for you. But you can't complain, "Life is not giving me a fair shake," or "Rain Drops Keep Falling on My Head." Where does that get you? You must look for solutions.

You have to be like the O'Jays, that old R&B group who sang: "Ain't No Stopping Us Now."

Your attitude has to be that specific, that strong.

If you want to increase your pay, your goal should not just be a raise, or "I want to make a lot of money." It should be a specific amount of increase. You must fix your mind on exactly what you want so you can take specific steps to get it and the self-conscious mind can take control.

Then the question is: What do you intend to give in compensation for the money? There's no such thing as something for nothing.

So you should aspire for something exact. That's how you light your path.

And once that path is illuminated, you get real ambitions. And then your desire increases with each success. All that is about attitude.

Figuratively speaking, success goes all the way up to the two hundredth floor. You can get off on any floor you want. It takes more effort to get to the top than it does to, say, the seventy-fifth floor. And you can be sure an attitude of commitment is what will get you higher and higher.

Someone said that people are afraid of hard work. I believe it is more that people don't know what hard work is. There was a time when people worked really hard because there were so many jobs available.

Now you have to be able to work hard and smart. The dynamics—the economy, ever-changing technology—require many workers to change jobs every five years or so. So an attitude of adapting has to be a part of your psyche now.

Let's Clap It Up

Enthusiasm, to me, equates to a passion for work and life. It makes everything we do a labor of love. And it's only common sense that our efforts to accomplish any task will be more rewarding if our accomplishments are born of love, rather than a job or chore. If you really want to succeed, the journey to do so is much more pleasant when you are involved in something you have a real desire to do.

That leads you to have enthusiasm for the job or situation, which means you will naturally put more effort into it.

Think about it: A job does not feel like a job when you are engaged in a project or occupation you enjoy.

I learned this lesson early in life, through my love of sports. I played basketball as a child because of my love for the game. I never had a problem motivating myself to practice my skills on the basketball court. Playing was a joy, a treat, which was a reason I excelled.

Putting in time to get better was not a task; it was a pleasure.

Contrast that with my daily chores on the family farm: feeding the pigs, milking the cows, and mending fences. I never did become an expert at these tasks, but I did them well because that was my attitude—do your best.

Of course, my parents taught me the value of hard work, and the sense of self-discipline and pride they instilled in me provided sufficient motivation for me to do my chores at a high level of competence. I just never had a passion for these tasks. They were never my true calling.

Sports were my greatest love, and so I had double the self-discipline and enthusiasm when it came to basketball than I did when it came to my chores. And when it came to going away to college, it was my ability on the basketball court that earned me the scholarship that helped launch my postcollege life.

In coaching my basketball team at Richmond High School, I realized that I had to instill enthusiasm for the game as much as self-discipline if I wanted my players to reach their full potential. That's why I made sure that my practices included some fun activities along with all of the hard work. That's one reason I always held a scrimmage at the end of each practice session. The game of basketball itself is fun, and I always allowed my players to play the game, even in practice.

I was able to extend the same principles into the realm of education as well. I knew that my players would learn more, better, faster, if they had real enthusiasm for their schoolwork along with self-discipline. Whenever we traveled to a basketball tournament in another town, I always tried to include something in the trip that would add to my players' enthusiasm for learning.

On one trip, we visited a black history museum; some of the kids had never been to any kind of museum at all. As any good educator will tell you, there are even more opportunities outside of the classroom for instilling enthusiasm for learning in young people than there are in the classroom.

Coaching After Richmond High

After seven years, I left Richmond High in 2006 so that I could coach on a larger arena—the world. I became a public speaker, addressing many Fortune 500 companies around the world, sharing my message of inspiration and commitment and teamwork.

But after a few years on the speaking circuit, I took

some time out to coach a team in a new sport called SlamBall. Developed by Mason Gordon for Tollin/Robbins Productions, SlamBall was basketball played on trampolines, with some rule adjustments to take into account the increased athleticism and physicality with which the game was played.

When Mike Tollin, Brian Robbins, and Mason Gordon first approached me and described to me their new sport, I was hooked. Imagine a basketball game where the players can literally fly ten feet through the air or soar three feet above the basket with one bounce on the trampoline.

I was offered a chance to coach one of the first teams in the new SlamBall league that would be televised on the cable channel TNN, and I seized that opportunity with both hands. My instant enthusiasm for the new sport enabled me to approach the process of selecting my team in the league's initial draft. While other coaches focused on a player's college statistics when selecting their teams, I focused my efforts on finding players who displayed both great athleticism and a great enthusiasm and passion for the game. My goal was to find players whose enthusiasm for the sport matched my own.

Once I knew what I was looking for in my players, it was easy to find. In watching the players work out before the draft, I could always spot the ones who displayed their great enthusiasm for the game. You can tell these things in the way a player carries himself on the court.

He has a special skip in his stride that brings out his

love and pride in everything he says and does. When I had finished assembling my team, the Rumble, I knew that we had the makings of a champion team right from the start because all of my players loved the new Slam-Ball sport every bit as much as I did. And because they had that enthusiasm for the game, I knew they would accept the challenges I posed for them in practice in order to prepare them to excel.

I'm proud to say that the Rumble plowed through the other teams in the league, all the way to the very first championship in the history of SlamBall.

Obviously, all of our hard work in practice paid off in the games. But it wasn't just a case of my players having a positive self-image and great self-discipline, although they had both of those. I firmly believe that it was my players' enthusiasm for the sport itself that played a major role in that championship season. And because I shared their enthusiasm, I was able to communicate with them and lead them more effectively as their head coach.

Our mutual enthusiasm enabled us to execute this remarkably exciting sport in a dynamic and flamboy-ant style that delighted the live and TV audiences alike. SlamBall scored great TV ratings successes right from the start, and the Rumble, with me at the helm, led the way in garnering the highest ratings of them all.

Our success in that league basically is a case study in how enthusiasm is a key quality for anyone who hopes for success in life or business. Your true path should be led by your passion, although I am aware of the millions of people who are in jobs because they sought the highest salary.

Even at that, success can be achieved in large quantities by virtue of being persistent about whatever endeavor is in your path. Persistence means not accepting less than required.

That persistence has to be guided by an attitude of commitment, meaning landmines will be averted at all costs. And all that should be fortified with an enthusiasm that permeates your being—and anyone who comes in contact with you—and charges a dogged determination to get the job accomplished.

Chapter Seven

Courage Counts

I walked into the gym at Richmond High for the first time as the new basketball coach resplendent in suit and tie. Acknowledgments of my school records as a basketball player there hung high on the walls. I had a swagger, as they say now, a gait that exuded confidence.

Inside, I was scared.

I had never coached before on a high school level. Sure, it was my alma mater, but it was a much different time. The kids were damaged by the conditions. They were harder, tougher, more cynical, and less trusting. They did not know who I was and they did not care.

I had to call on courage to take on a job I had not done before in a place that required so much more than teaching basketball. But the courage was there for me to tap into because I had succeeded in other aspects of my life, so I had a reservoir of confidence on which to draw my courage.

That's how it works. When you are confident in what you are doing, when you have faith, you can have the courage to do what is needed.

No one has ever achieved success without having the courage to take their dreams and make them a reality.

So what then is courage? It is the ability to confront your deepest fear and move forward despite that fear. No one is fearless. We all have our doubts. Courage is that quality of character that enables us to surpass our doubts and fears and achieve our highest aspirations in the face of seemingly insurmountable odds.

Remember the story from the Bible of David and Goliath. Goliath was the champion of the Philistines, a giant of a warrior who thought he was invincible. But David, a mere boy, had the courage to stand against him in battle, and he defeated Goliath with his sling and a single stone. But it was really David's courage that defeated Goliath. To overcome the greatest of obstacles, you must be prepared to face that obstacle with all the courage in your heart.

Perhaps the biggest fear for everyone is the fear of failure. No one wants to fail. No one likes to fail. But all of us will fail from time to time. In fact, if you look at many of the great people in history, they sometimes failed more than once before achieving greatness.

Abraham Lincoln is a good example. He failed at every business venture he ever tried before he became a lawyer. He even failed at politics. But through all of his failures he never lost the courage of his convictions. Those convictions eventually led to his famous debates with Senator Stephen A. Douglas, and it was those debates where he became famous and buoyed his election as President of the United States at a crucial time in our nation's history. Our country is a better place because of President Lincoln's courage.

That is what separates those who succeed from those who do not succeed: The people who make a success of themselves are not afraid to fail.

It is important to note that courage is a skill that can be learned and developed through careful planning. The most direct way to develop your courage is to identify your deepest fear and then confront it with direct action. By overcoming your fear, you will acquire the courage you need to attain your goals in life.

To beat your fear, you must confront your fear. Take a moment and write down the thing you fear the most. Is it starting a new job? Asking for a raise? Calling a beautiful woman and making a date? Speaking in front of a group of executives?

Write it down, and bring it out of your mind and into the real world, where you can begin to confront your fear. Force yourself to undertake the challenge. Will you still be afraid? Yes, of course. But courage is taking action despite your fear. And once you've taken action, you'll find that your fear can be overcome.

Through courage, we purge ourselves of the paralysis that comes out of fear. And we learn that our fears in real life are never as powerful as they are when they're only inside our minds.

I am now a public speaker in high demand, but I still have my doubts and fears about getting up in front of an audience of strangers. Such doubts and fears are the most natural thing in the world. To overcome mine, I like to practice my speeches in front of my mirror. I also like to talk into a tape recorder and play the speeches back to myself, so I can hear myself speak.

With each practice speech, I cultivate my courage to make my real speech in front of an audience. By the time I do appear before the public, I've made my speech about a hundred times. And with my newfound confidence, I have the ability to add to my speech right during the middle of it as I tailor my words in response to the reaction of my audience. My confidence is the direct result of my courage.

I have seen courage and been courageous at times of my life that really matter.

Witnessing Courage

Perhaps the most vivid example of courage I witnessed was from one of my players in 1999, the first year I coached at Richmond High.

We'll call this kid Mac and he was something special. I first met Mac when I went into a classroom to check on another player. I noticed him sitting there in the front row.

I left the class and I thought about it: His head was at my shoulders—and he was sitting down. As the basketball coach, that size mattered. So, I went back into the classroom and had a conversation with him.

"What's your name, young man?" I asked.

He said his name, but I could hardly hear him.

"Do you play basketball?" I asked.

"No," he said in that barely audible voice. He would not look at me in the eye.

"Well, looks like you are a tall young man. I would like you to come out to practice."

"My mom won't let me play," he mumbled.

He was six-foot-four, one hundred eighty pounds. That height for a high school team was important, so I really wanted him to come out to practice. The first time he did not show. But he did the second time.

The thing about Mac was that his family really had nothing. And when I say nothing, I mean nothing. He was a good kid, but his family was broke. They were living from motel to motel and off whatever the church could do for them. It was that bad.

His father was nowhere to be found and his mom tried hard, but it was a real struggle.

The young man was lacking in self-esteem; he hardly spoke and no one spoke to him. He came to school with literally no money for lunch and was not dressed in the most fashionable clothes.

There was every reason for him to quit and be a problem child.

But Mac and his sister kept coming to school. Most kids would just give up. He and his sister were as courageous as anyone I have ever encountered. He was sitting in front of the class, which told me he had a desire to learn. That took courage because he was there for all to see that his family could not afford him the most fashionable clothes.

His mom actually let him play and the transformation that he went through was amazing. Seeing the courage in him made me a better person.

He had never played basketball, but his effort was excellent. He gave me everything he had. And once he started learning the game and its terminology, he started to show gradual progress.

I used to look at him in amazement because it took courage for him to even agree to come out for the team. This was a team of very good players, players who laughed at you if you didn't know what you were doing. They laughed about his clothes and shoes. He took it all.

For about six weeks the kids made fun of him, and he did not offer a retort; he just kept working. His teammates didn't want to pair with him in drills at practice because if you lost, you had to run. He was just terrible when he joined the team. He couldn't make a layup from right under the basket.

But he always asked what he could do to get better. He was determined. I paid attention and I saw that he started to believe in himself. He had to see someone else believe in him before he could see his own virtues.

Mac had virtually nothing. But we never talked about his condition. We went on a week-long trip for a tournament and he had fifty cents in his pocket and a sandwich. That was it—for a *week-long* trip.

And he wasn't going to say anything. He was just going to endure it. He was full of pride and class and I didn't want to insult him or put him in an awkward position by just giving him money. But I was not going to let him starve, so I gave him duties that allowed him to earn some extra dollars.

So we went on this trip, and while he had progressed as a player, he still only played when we were comfortably in front and he still was pretty withdrawn. On the way to the tournament, he hardly said a thing.

On the way back, we couldn't shut him up.

Being on the team in general changed his life, and that trip in particular was the moment we could see it.

We played the first game in the tournament and were up by about thirty points. I put him in and we were passing him the ball so he could score the first-ever points of his career.

But it was like there was a lid on the basket. He could not make a layup. He was clumsy and awkward. He must have taken fifteen shots. But he did not score.

During the next game, we got up big again, and I put him in the game once more. It was so obvious that we wanted him to score so badly that the other team's fans wanted him to score, too. It was almost like the other team was passing him the ball.

I watched him out there, and all I could think about were the trials he had been through: moving from motel to motel with his mom and sister; jumping from school to school; not having any financial resources; not having any clothes like the other kids wore; being shy and lacking self-esteem; enduring all the jokes about his appearance and his inability to play basketball.

He took all that—and the grueling physical requirements that came with it—and had the courage to fight on.

I thought about all that when he scored his first points in a basketball game, which was the reason I jumped probably twenty feet in the air. Everyone in the gym felt good for him. He ended up scoring ten points. It was amazing.

Mac made us feel good as a team. And everyone could see how great he felt about himself.

That bus ride back home was an incredible experience. This kid who was an introvert talked and talked and talked. He had found himself.

Instead of sitting there observing his teammates or looking out the window as he had on the way to the game, he was loud and laughing on the way back, participating in the usual teenage hijinks that occur on a team bus.

"How you like me now?" he yelled over and over. And he shared in jokes and generally had as much fun as anyone. It was hard to believe that this was the same kid who'd only softly mumbled a few words when I first met him.

I could tell he truly felt he was part of the team because he contributed points in a game. His self-worth was instantly lifted.

Later, I remember when Mac got his first dunk in a game. I went in my office after the game, closed the door, and started crying. That's how much his rise on the team and as a person had affected me.

The courage he showed to overcome his circumstances and be a beacon of light for his younger sister was amazing. And it was not just basketball. Basketball gave him something to do and helped him get into shape and socialize in the process.

But it was really about how courageous and how committed Mac was to his education. He never missed school. And this is someone who did not have money to pay for the bus. He walked to and from school no matter what motel his family was staying at.

He understood that the quickest way to have something was education. I feel like not only did he change his life, but he changed mine because I saw what courage really was.

After that game, he was confident, and you saw him walk with his head up, shoulders back. All the odds were against him—he should not have graduated from high school or even attempted to go to college. But our team and coaching staff surrounded that kid.

There were times when I said to myself, "No way he would keep going." But you could see that light burning in him.

Now the young man works at Coca-Cola, has a wife and two kids, and is the ultimate father. You want courage, that's what courage is—maintaining, fighting, persevering in the face of fear to get where you believe you should be.

Confronting the Bully

That kid had many routes he could have taken, and in Richmond, California, one of them was to become a drug dealer. I'm convinced, because he was in such need of money, that he would have turned to drugs if he were not on our basketball team.

That was true about most of our players, which meant I had to take a proactive approach to make sure they did not stray. Although they were good kids, they saw the results of the drug trade every day. The big fancy cars and ostentatious jewelry, admiration from misguided locals.

At that time, in the late nineties, the drug trade was a huge business in Richmond. It was and continues to be one of the horrible elements that made the city notorious. With the rampant drug trade and drug use came crime and death at a rate so fast that the kids became almost numb to it.

It drove me absolutely crazy that these drug dealers who came from Richmond, who knew the parents of the kids they had working for them or were selling to, would poison their own community without so much as a hesitation. I was trying to help kids, and finally I just couldn't take the idea of their falling off that deep end. I summoned all the courage I had in me and found the location of the town's drug kingpin and went to him for a talk.

I was not scared, as I had dealt with other drug dealers in the past, but I was concerned. However, sometimes when something means so much to you, your level of courageousness elevates without fear. So in my daily attire of suit and tie, I went over there to a place that was something like you would see in a movie from some years ago, *New Jack City.*

This drug kingpin had taken over a building in the projects. And when I approached, several of his lieutenants stopped me and patted me down, checking for weapons.

When they did not find one, a guy said: "What are you doing here? Don't you know everyone has a gun?"

I said, "For what I came to accomplish today, I don't need a gun." Eventually, they let me in to see the kingpin. I was in this room that was nicely decorated—totally unlike what I expected. I was talking to this guy who looked just as I expected—bandanna on his head, T-shirt, gaudy gold chain.

He and I had a few words and then, after about thirty seconds, this big chair with a high back that was behind a desk facing the wall rotated toward me. I thought I had been talking to the kingpin, but I had not. It was one of his underlings.

The kingpin looks at me and says, "Coach Carter. I just saw you on the news this morning. Good to see you."

I was shocked. He was there all along, listening. And I was amazed by this guy. He was dressed in a navy blue suit, a crisp white shirt, and a red necktie, as if he were going to work for a Fortune 500 company. Again, I couldn't believe it.

He extended his hand for me to shake, but I didn't. I have a philosophy: I don't put my hand in, well, let's say, feces. He just looked at me and we went on with the business I came for.

He sat there very calm and collected—probably because he had several armed guys around him that served as bodyguards. He was an articulate man, about twenty-two, twenty-three years old, who exuded supreme confidence.

Immediately, he knew who I was although I had not seen the young man before.

"Coach Carter, what are you doing here? Aren't you supposed to be on the other side of the tracks?" he said.

I told him, "I grew up here. This is my home. I live in this community."

But I understood his point—I was as far away as you could be from a drug lord's turf. Looking back on it now, it's almost as if I were crazy to confront that man in that manner on his turf. But I had a single-minded focus and really did not give it much thought.

It turned out that he had graduated from Richmond High and college before making that career decision. He was a fan of our team.

I was concerned about going to visit this guy, but I was not meek. I knew he considered any kid around to be fair game for him. That's just how it was. He had taken over.

Still, I told him that those gentlemen on my team were trying to do something with their lives and I wasn't going to stand for them being a part of his drug team. I told him they were off limits.

He looked at me and smiled. "I respect what you're

saying, Coach," he said. "I won't recruit those boys. But they are stars in the city right now and so they would make good runners for me."

Amazing, because I had a similar response from the drug dealer I met in Richmond. I realized that even drug dealers had a marketing plan. But my kids were not going to be a part of it. I had no choice. I could not be a coward and sit back and allow God knows what to happen to these kids under my watch. That alone drove my courage to a place where I could go into that drug hellhole to make a case with the city's most notorious drug dealer.

"You're doing a wonderful job," he said. "I respect that and I respect you coming here. But just like you have a business and are doing a service to the community, I'm running a business and serving the community.

"So I won't go after them, as long as they are on your team and stay in school. But if they slip up, they're mine."

It was really an interesting and sad twenty minutes with this guy. Here was someone who was smart and had every skill set to be legitimately successful. And yet that was not his choice. I could not leave there without finding out how he became a drug dealer.

"It was a conscious choice," he said, and left it at that.

Maybe someone got to him as a kid. Drug pushers would plant money on you to give you a taste of what having it felt like, the hope being that you would like it and want more. It happened to me, but I just threw the money on the ground and kept going. I wasn't tempted.

But these kids knew drug dealers and saw the material things they bought with their dirty money, so they were more susceptible to the allure.

"You seem to be a very educated man. You got your education," I said. "Let them get theirs."

He complimented me on my suit and my success with the team and pretty much moved past my inquiry about his career choice. And that was fine. I was there to protect my team.

I learned that other athletes in the area who had been stars at one time were selling drugs. I would ride down the street and someone would point out, "See that guy right there? That's so-and-so, who was a high school All-American." And I would be amazed. "That's him?" I'd ask, shocked that a former star athlete would end up a drug dealer.

There were so many bad, negative examples all around, all the time. That let me know I had to take measures.

My thinking was that if one of my kids fell through the cracks and looked successful on the other side, the illegal drug trade side, it would make the other kids think it was the thing to do, or at least okay to do. And I couldn't have that.

The way those kids had galvanized the town with what we were doing on the basketball court, the community embraced them. They were perceived as winners. So there was no decision for me; it had to be done.

I'm grateful that none of my kids slipped. Not one.

That's a credit to them, not me. But I knew I could not

sit back and allow the possibility to be freely there for them. I had to summon the strength and the courage to push the negative stuff into a corner or it was going to push me into a corner.

They probably realize this now, but not then: They were one bad decision away from destroying their lives. That's all it takes—one mistake. But they were all courageous to not succumb to the elements. Bad things were there for them: drugs, drug use, crime. But they believed that a better day was coming. They wanted something good for themselves.

COACH CARTER CARROT

When you do all the right things for all the right reasons, it gives you courage. And those kids had it.

Chapter Eight

Embracing Hard Work

When I opened Carter's Sporting Goods Store in Richmond in 1984, I leased a small upstairs space at Market Square Mall at the corner of Harbor Way and McDonald. Don't let the name fool you. It was in an underwhelming little strip mall of about a dozen stores probably ten minutes from the school.

The store was located in a decent neighborhood of working-class people, but being upstairs afforded me virtually no foot traffic. So no one passing my business knew I was there, which, of course, impacted my sales.

That locale actually was the impetus that sparked my commitment to put all I had into the business to make it successful. I was working from a disadvantage with my location, so in order to compensate, I had to work extremely hard to generate customers.

And so I used signage on the street to let people

know I was there. I became a social butterfly, joining the local Police Athletic League, the local Small Business Association, the Chamber of Commerce, the Boys and Girls Club board. I put myself in as many positions as possible to meet potential clients and supporters.

On top of that, my work had to be heads above the competition. And it was. I was able to do what my competitors did and more—and for a more reasonable rate because my overhead was less.

The results were phenomenal.

My business grew rapidly, and when the store next to me closed, the owner of the building knocked down the wall and I was able to expand the size of my store. All that did was give me more incentive to get it done. I redoubled my efforts, and in six months, I outgrew that space. Another wall was taken out and another wall, and at that point, it didn't make sense for me to continue to grow upstairs, even though my store was now attracting business to the other stores at the mall.

Not only had I drawn attention to my own store, but I was creating foot traffic for the other businesses as well. As people were coming into my store, I'd tell them about the other businesses in the mall, which made me a real commodity. Finally, a large space that would work for me opened up downstairs. But the rent would triple. It was quite a leap to go from 800 square feet to 2,000 square feet. But the owner was a good businessman and he knew losing me as a tenant would not be a smart move. My store's name had spread through the community as *the* place to go for your sporting goods needs, and I added real value to the area because waves of people were coming to the mall. I was firmly established as a strong fixture in the community.

That success was about my work ethic more than anything else. I was never the cheapest, but I did a quality job for a reasonable rate. And I delivered. I called it underpromising and overdelivering, meaning I would not build up expectations for something I could not execute. That was the worst thing any business owner could do—disappoint a customer. So I would know what I could produce and when I could produce it. I made my deadline, which made my customers believe in Carter's Sporting Goods.

Oftentimes I slept at my store to complete orders that required my time after hours. One time, I had this huge order of customized T-shirts that had to be the right color. But I just could not get the ink right. I had to mix combinations of colors over and over until I found the right mix. I had promised those T-shirts in the morning, and so I stayed up all night until I got the color perfect and all the shirts made just as the client expected. I was exhausted, but it was a rewarding exhaustion because I had fulfilled the order just as I'd promised.

Being that reliable and efficient made my business the steak on the block, not the chicken. We were an upgrade from any competition. And the people respected that and kept coming back. Word of mouth was a huge ally. People talked about the services I provided and referred others, helping my business grow.

But it was important that I went into business with a

plan, with focus. I went to every seminar I could find about starting a business. I befriended everyone in the community who had been in business, to learn about the buying habits of the people, the traffic, the marketing schemes they implemented that worked—and those that did not work, because you can learn from the bad as well as the good.

You can have all the theory in the world, but having worked for Mr. Dunkley and Mr. Cartwright as a youth was really significant because I saw their work ethic and business practices. That practical experience was invaluable, and when I had questions about my business, I called on them. Lots of times in business you will have bad days and the owner will just shut down. But I had resources to call on for aid, advice, and strategies. However, they can only help you if they know you need help. Sometimes pride gets in the way and business owners wait too long to seek assistance.

In the end, your business is about what you put into it. Time and effort should never be a concern.

Do What You Say You Would Do

Nothing disappoints a consumer more than not receiving what he spends his hard-earned money on. So to avoid that disappointment—and the possibility of bad news traveling fast—I was adamant about getting it right and on time. Jobs that took my competition three days to complete many times took me one. People wanted stuff when they wanted stuff, so my word was bond. I made sure it was right and ready when I said it would be right and ready.

My clients would say, "Wow, we can get these custom T-shirts back the next day?"

And I made sure they did.

Not delivering is one of the most common and biggest problems in business. Simply put, you must produce when you committed to producing. No way around it. Some so-called business owners would say just about anything to get your business, which is underhanded— and will doom their business if they do not deliver because, as I mentioned before, bad news seems to spread faster than good news.

It was good news to my clients when they could reach me at any time. I was always accessible. I had my business phone calls transferred to my cell phone when I was not in the store or after hours.

I did anything to separate myself from my competitors. And my efficiency, the quality of my work, and my accessibility helped me go from having no major contract to several.

It also helped that I developed a system that made ordering our products simple. I streamlined the process so customers were in and out and did not have to spend a lot of time mired in paperwork.

I wasn't in business just to be in business. I was in it to make a living—and to make a mark. Some start in business to say they have a business or to give it a try. They hang up a sign and they are happy. I, meanwhile, had to feed my family. I had nothing else to fall back on, so I had no choice but to make it work. I invested my savings, begged and borrowed money to get it up and running. That might sound dramatic, but it is true. Family and friends helped out a lot. And that kind of investment made my business a commitment that was as much emotional as it was financial. My store was a part of me. It was my passion. People I cared about expected me to deliver something special, and I was not about to let them down.

So I became a true entrepreneur. I knew my profit margins and my inventory. Most important, I knew what people wanted through conversing with them inside and outside the store. I thought it was good business to know my customers and their desires, and that allowed me to stock my store with inventory I knew spoke to who they were and what they liked.

But there was another big difference between me and others who supplied the same products. I was so knowledgeable about my inventory and deliverability that I always expressed an intelligent opinion based on that knowledge. A customer might say, "That other guy is two dollars cheaper. I would respond: "But he won't have it ready until Saturday. I can have it for you tomorrow."

In the grand scheme of things, people want what they want when they want it. I understood and embraced that notion, to the point where I almost always made the deadline the customer desired.

COACH CARTER CARROT

I always talked about the benefits of my products. Others talked about features, like having Air Force One sneakers in multiple colors. That's fine. But I would tell the mother who was shopping for her son that the shoe provided great support and that you could take out the insole and put it in the washer to get out that funky sneaker smell. And the mother would say, "Oh, really? I didn't know that. That's the shoe I want, then, because I can't stand that smell."

Delivering by the deadline went a long way with my customers, and it was one of the reasons about ninety percent of my clients returned to my store for more purchases. I gave them what they wanted when they wanted it, and that helped me gain a connection to them. I also understood people do business with people they like, so I established relationships and treated everyone who came through my door with respect.

I wore a suit and tie every day and I offered "yes sir" to males and "yes ma'am" to females. That level of customer service cannot be underestimated. I made my store a place where consumers felt comfortable and their business was appreciated. I knew many of my customers had had experiences similar to mine, when I went into a business and the workers there either ignored me or made me feel like they didn't want me there. And I would inevitably leave without spending my money because of that level of discomfort.

I never understood how business owners felt it was okay to follow customers in stores or not greet them pleasantly when they entered the store or showed their gratitude for their business. That's exactly how you fail.

The Right Mentality

Do you know what kept me working hard every day? I was scared to fail. I had no other options. Well, of course I could do something else if I had to. But my mind-set was that failure was not an option.

And when you have that mentality, you are inspired to make things happen.

I always considered myself a winner. I had made a decision that I wanted to own a sporting goods shop. Period. I had studied a mockup of a store in college. I was pursing my worthwhile goal.

And that goal was born when I was young. I remember being on Market Street in San Francisco as a kid and seeing men dressed in suits walking into offices with a *Wall Street Journal* tucked under their arms. That excited me.

The other thing that kept me determined was that was all I knew: hard work. In fact, I actually had no idea it was called "hard work." It was just a way of life for me, from childhood. It was something we did as a family, all of us. It wasn't considered anything beyond that. I didn't know anything differently from putting my all into everything I did.

That definitely came from my parents. I saw them get up and work ten, twelve hours a day and then come home and work on our farm. Witnessing that told me that was how it is done. You put your work in.

I might be a country boy, but that upbringing gave me a foundation, a strong work ethic. I see many businesses fail from a lack of intensity, a lack of drive. If you do not put everything into it, it is unrealistic to expect much out of it. I ran my business as I played basketball—with a fervor and commitment. I went at it hard. There were no designated work hours for me. I just worked until the job was done and until we were set up to make it happen the next day, too.

You put in that kind of effort and it will create business opportunities. And then, of course, you have to embrace the opportunities if you want to advance. And embracing the opportunity means putting everything into it for it to thrive. That's what it always comes back to: work. In the end, the success or failure comes down to you, the business owner.

Here's one of my laws: I don't accept any excuses because I don't make any. If you give people wiggle room, you know what they do? They wiggle. I put in the work so there's no room to offer excuses, wiggles, or anything else.

In all my years of coaching, never had one player missed practice. The only way they could miss practice was if they were dead, and they knew that. So they showed up.

And of all the players I coached, my son, Damien, was the hardest worker. He was determined to be first in all drills in practice. He hustled. He lifted weights. He refined his game. He became a student of the game.

As my son, I think he always had something to prove—to me, to his teammates, and to himself. To me, because I was a very gifted athlete and he was my offspring, and so he wanted to prove to me that he was equally skilled. It turned out that he broke all the records I set at Richmond High. So he showed me and himself at the same time.

He was also adamant about proving to his teammates that he deserved whatever he received because they certainly thought he had favor as my son. It was natural for them to look at him as less than them—he transferred into the school and they did not know him. But they came to admire his effort and eventually follow his lead on how hard you have to work to be successful.

My son inherited from me a burning desire for achievement. That's what drives us. Some people get on a treadmill of failure, going about business the wrong way, unwilling to put in the work, and not knowing how to provide quality services in a timely fashion.

Sometimes business isn't bad; it's that the people running it are doing bad business. If you get in the habit of doing things the right way, it becomes a routine to create a successful environment.

Getting Ready to Work

Get this: To be successful, you must prepare to be successful, prepare to do the job. That goes two ways. Here's one:

We had a mule on our farm that knew his way to a watering hole to get water and come back. He was conditioned and could do it on his own. But my dad made me walk with the mule to where he had to go and back. You know why? Because I had to be doing something. He was growing a worker, preparing me to be accustomed to working.

The same amount of time should be dedicated to preparing to work as it does to performing the actual work. That was always my thought process. Before we had practices, I had already outlined the entire two hours, down to the minute. So we were efficient and did not waste time. We made the most of our time, in fact.

Think about it: When your job is to cut down a tree, most people go in and grab an ax and start chopping. I would spend forty-five minutes or so sharpening the ax, so the job of chopping the tree would be easier because my tool was properly prepared to do the job.

It's about staying on the ready, putting yourself in a position to succeed. Being organized. People who are organized are confident. They have their plans in order, their inventory, their strategy. They can move forward knowing they are set up for success.

These days you can't just work hard anymore. You have to combine hard work with deft planning to flourish in business. I never looked at business as a job; it was always about a career. When you look at it that way, everything has more purpose because you focus on building your skills and sustaining for an extended period instead of having in your head the idea that "It's just a job and I can find a new one any time." See how noncommittal that sounds?

Some people like to wish their way to success. They hope something good happens as opposed to *making* things happen. I willed my way to success. I worked my way to success. I prepared my way to success.

Changing the Game Plan

Flexibility is the ability to change course in midstream when you find that your chosen path isn't working as well as you thought it would. Flexibility gives you the options of reshaping your commitment and revising your game plan to achieve your goals. Often, there's more than one way to end up at a desired destination. What works for one person may not work for another. By maintaining maximum flexibility, you radically increase your chances of achieving success in life.

Here's what flexibility is not: It isn't abandoning your goals because you think they're too hard to reach. It isn't giving up self-discipline because your chosen road has proven to be rockier than you first expected. Flexibility is about seizing opportunities as they arise. As each of us goes about our journey through life, numerous opportunities for success will cross our paths. But do we have the flexibility of mind to recognize such opportunities? And do we have the flexibility of method to shape our game plan to take into account new information as it becomes available to us?

When I first became the basketball coach at Richmond High School, some of the star players from the previous year's team were reluctant to play for me. They heard about the contract I was asking all of my players to sign, and they felt that I was too much of a disciplinarian for them to continue in their old, me-first patterns of behavior. Well, they were right about that, but there was nothing I could do at first if I wanted them on my team. I didn't want selfish players on my squad. I wanted winners dedicated to team ball, not individuals always looking out for themselves.

As you can imagine, my first team wasn't blessed with a lot of talent. So I had to change my game plan to suit the particular talents of my players. Our strengths were our depth and our commitment to fundamental team basketball. I decided to make conditioning and defense the focus of my practices. I might not have the most talented team, but I would have a team that could play flat-out hard-nosed ball for thirty-two minutes each night.

It was not my usual style of play, but I had the flexibility of mind to introduce a new style of play which best suited our personnel. We won our first six games that year. Our hallmark was wearing our opponents down over the course of the game with nonstop, in-your-face defense. And we ran the full length of the court at every opportunity, taking advantage of our depth and conditioning. After the first six games, the star players from the season before saw that the team could win without them, and they all quickly signed my contract and made a commitment to playing basketball the Ken Carter way.

I have many examples from my life where flexibility of mind enabled me to achieve success by taking a different path than I had foreseen as the surest way of achieving my goals. When I was coaching the Rumble in SlamBall, I was able to draft the two best big men in the league, Dion Mays and David Redmond. But these two players turned out to be so competitive with each other that I found I couldn't play them both at the same time. I hit upon the solution of using them in tandem, one at a time.

By dividing their minutes and alternating their play, I turned their natural competitive desires into a plus, since each one of them was motivated to play his best in place of the other in order to prove to me that he deserved the most minutes. I had not planned on this system of substitution when I created my team, but by remaining flexible I discovered the best lineup to maximize the overall performance of the team.

Accepting "No" Is a Mistake

When I first started selling the movie *Coach Carter* in Hollywood, I was told that for a beginner like myself I

should give my story over to a more experienced producer and let them do the work of selling the picture to
a studio. I met with several established producers and
entrusted one of them with my life story. Unfortunately,
this producer was unable to sell my story to the studios.
In fact, after a period of three months he told me flat out
that it couldn't be done.

I reviewed my situation at that point and decided that
what I needed was a change of direction. All my adult
life I had run a string of small businesses, and if I had
any skill at all, it was the skill to sell. I had the ability
to sell myself as a competent and dedicated business-
person who could give the customer what he wanted.
I decided to rely on these same skills when it came to
selling my life story to Hollywood. I wrote up my story
in a treatment form, made up a booklet and other tools
to enhance my presentation, and then tried to sell my
story myself, directly to the studios. I was able to secure
my meetings with Paramount Pictures and MTV Films,
and they bought my story.

I had found roadblocks thrown up in my path to success, but I had the presence of mind and quality of character to travel down a different path. This is what I mean
by flexibility. I never lost sight of the ultimate goal: to
sell my life story and turn it into a Hollywood movie.
But when I found my efforts blocked as I executed my
game plan, I switched gears and found another way to
get it done.

Flexibility is one of the core qualities of character for
anyone who wants to achieve success. Sometimes our

first plan is not always our best plan. Sometimes God or fate throws us a curve, and we have to adjust our swing to hit the ball out of the park. By maintaining maximum flexibility, we enhance our chances for success.

Like any other quality of character, flexibility can be developed and refined. Flexibility is a skill that you build up with the right efforts. When you set your goal, think of every path possible to help you reach that goal. You might be surprised to find that there is often more than one way to achieve your heart's desire. Never be afraid to try something different. You never know if a new direction will turn out to be the right direction.

But you have to explore all opportunities. That's a part of having a commitment to hard work. You do not accept "no," you grind it out despite obstacles, and you adjust to get to the desired destination.

Chapter Nine

Doing Things the Right Way

Before I could get settled comfortably in my office at Richmond High, my team and I were considered underdogs. And based on the dynamics working against us, I understood why.

The doubters were quite vocal about what we would *not* do. They looked at some obvious issues and came to the definitive position that winning was out of the question. After all, we were a basketball team with no basketballs. There were no nets on the goals. In fact, all the comforts of a traditional high school basketball team—working showers, uniforms, to name just a few— we did not have.

What we did have was my commitment to elevating the tangible (gear, towels, supplies, etc.) and intangible (a culture of inadequacy). It was like taking over a company that was floundering with low morale. It needed an overhaul.

There was hardly anyone I encountered who believed we could amount to anything worth anyone's attention. What I heard was basically, "Just quit right now because you're not going to get anywhere."

If I were a weak person, I would have been influenced by those people's expectations of doom. But I had a faith. The naysayers' consistent words of discouragement actually made me more determined to stay and reverse things.

One of the things working against me was the dynamics of the city of Richmond. In 1997 when I came on board, and even now, it is one of the most dangerous cities in America. Drugs and gangs are prominent. And when those two evil brothers are together, crime and death play prominent roles—and a culture of oppression exists. In this case, the kids were resistant to change, hardened by their circumstances and not particularly optimistic about their futures.

They believed they were underdogs, that life did not have much to offer them and that their prospects in basketball were limited.

At Richmond High when I coached there, half of the students did not graduate—an alarming statistic. Even more alarming was the fact that eighty percent of the students were more likely to go to jail than to graduate. Those facts made the challenge far more important than just basketball, although my plan was to use basketball as the vehicle for bringing about change in the kids in my program.

People often said to me, "Coach Carter, the kids won't like you." I told them, "That's okay. I don't need a fifteen-year-old friend. I need these kids to be productive people, so they can enter the workforce."

The journey from underdog to top dog was exactly like a long highway trip. On a highway you come across various signs, such as YIELD, SLIPPERY WHEN WET, DIVIDED HIGHWAY, WATCH FOR ICE, ROAD BLOCKED, DETOUR—and we encountered all that en route to "top dog."

Sometimes we had to apply the brakes. We had to refill our gas tank. We had to accelerate. We had to weave through traffic and endure many potholes. Sometimes we came to a complete stop, rested, and continued on the journey.

That's just the way it is when you try to do something great. Obstacles, big and small, appear. And the best way to attack them is with faith in what you are doing.

I have this definition for the word "believe":

Because
Every
Living
Individual
Excels
Victoriously
Every time

That definition is all about faith, the ability to believe when others don't believe in you. I believed in my team, even though they did not believe in themselves, so I had to transfer that faith from me to them. I could see in them that they were not losers, even as they viewed themselves that way. I actually saw them as potential leaders.

And that is where you can make a dent when building a team or staff. Instill confidence, which is not always easy. As the leader of the underdogs, I developed exercises such as the public speaking responsibility I mentioned earlier and challenged them in the classroom; when they got better in those areas, their confidence in themselves increased, too.

But with a basketball team, the best way to make it believe in itself is to win on the basketball court. My method was to create a competitive atmosphere that would become a culture. So I developed competitions in practice to build their sense of value of winning. I created games they would play within the scheme of practice, games that they became adamant about winning, which built the team's overall desire to be victorious.

Additionally, I took a serious assessment of the talent I had. Everyone had strengths and weaknesses. My position was to give the weaknesses less attention than the strengths because strengths were something we could build on. And I learned that was a smart move because people are eager to get better in areas they are already good at over areas that require more work.

So I made my players who were strong ball-handlers become even stronger dribblers of the ball. Those players who were good at defense, I worked with them to be superior at defense. Good rebounders became great rebounders. Stellar shooters became marksmen.

The result was a team of specialized talents that allowed me to use them in their areas of strength and to match them with teammates to give us what we needed at a particular point in the game. That's called assessing your talent and building your team. It should work exactly the same in business.

While constructing this unified group of players, we went through a lot of emotions from day to day, even from minute to minute, as they struggled with change and the idea that someone actually believed in their ability. It was emotional because the kids had no confidence in themselves or anyone else. They had been doing things for years one particular way; I wanted things done the *right* way. That was a culture change that was hard to implement.

At first, the players did not take practice seriously. They were not that interested in sharpening the areas of their games that were strong. They were not accustomed to giving the maximum effort. They thought they were good enough, even though they were not winning.

I had to teach them that the more they learned, the more they would be able to do—but that learning required doing it the right way. If you do not do it the right way, then you are not getting better.

The laws of the universe do not change for anyone. The laws of the universe are absolute. For instance: "What goes up must come down." It does not say which way it will come down, only that it will come down. Therefore, whatever it is that we do, if we do not learn it the right way, then we will not do it the right way.

There's Only One Way: The Right Way

Which begs the question: What is the right way? Simple, sort of. First, there has to be a commitment to the task, the project, the goal, which means there is a determination to put in the time and effort. If you used to run hard half of the time, you have to increase that to one hundred percent of the time.

If you worked out in the weight room for thirty minutes, you have to increase that to forty-five minutes. If you took one hundred shots a day, you must take two hundred shots a day. That's commitment. That's doing it the right way.

Another element would be to plan your course of action. Everything should start with a blueprint that should be well thought out and clear. It should be written down so you can refer to it at any point. It would be pointless to go into practice without the entire two hours broken down to the minute. That's what I did every day, and I posted the practice regimen on the door of the gym so the players could see it and understand what our goals were for the day. They were resistant at first. Then they came to rely on it because they understood that it provided structure and a layout of how their time would be spent.

Finally, doing it the right way requires embracing leadership. The first rule of thumb for anyone should be "I don't know everything." If you accept that notion, then you open yourself up to letting someone who knows more teach you.

Within my team and in business, you find individuals who are so used to doing it as they have done it that they just cannot believe someone could come along and teach them something new. Well, that's exactly what can and should happen. When you let go of the "I know everything" ideal, you embrace new offerings. And doing so opens you up to a new world, a world in which you can combine what you already know with what you learned to blossom in ways you hardly thought were imaginable.

A Faithful Journey

So, when I was finally able to get the team's ear, our transition from underdog to top dog had a real chance. It was one thing to hear the messages, the teachings, the demands. But it was another thing to get them to *listen*. Listening calls for absorption of information, and it wasn't until they began to listen that the evolution started to take shape.

In reality, they only heard the naysayers; they needed something to listen to that would alter their outlook. Having someone show confidence in them allowed them to gain an interest in proving the naysayers wrong.

Also, I listened to them—their concerns, their realities—which was something they were not accustomed to. By placing a value on their words, their thoughts and concerns, it helped us gain a connection and a trust.

Our team experienced a lot of feelings on our journey to becoming the top dog. The emotions expressed varied from day to day. I first instilled in them the emotion of desire. It started as a tiny spark, and as I added the fuel in their minds to want to do more and to be more, the spark ignited, and then spread until it became a burning desire to succeed. Once that desire burned in them, I channeled their thoughts to now have faith in themselves to get to the next step.

Faith is the opposite of fear. Many times people exhibit fear over faith because of a lack of knowledge. Remember what I said about general knowledge. It is no good until it is put in place, but you have to put it in the right place. I had to get the team to put their general knowledge in faith that we could do what the naysayers said we could not do.

There was no one star on our team; they were all shining stars to me. Teamwork was how we built success. The turning point in the team moving forward was them being organized. We set short-term goals like getting to the next class, which was a big step in the right direction. To be a good team member, you have to live according to the universe model.

My team did just that, and the journey of faith was set in motion. Whenever fear showed up, we pumped our muscles of faith even harder toward our goal. So now that we had the burning desire with faith, we could begin to hope for something more than we had. Any-

COACH CARTER CARROT

Watch your thoughts because they become your words. Watch your words because they become your actions. Watch your actions because they become your behavior. Watch your behavior because it becomes your future.

thing was better than what we had, which was a group of people who said we could not do it, a gym without any supplies, and a school district that did not support our vision. With hope (**h**elping **o**ur **p**eers **e**xcel), we were on our way to becoming the top dog.

Teamwork began to pay off, as their enthusiasm filled the air. The vision was now inside the players, even though they did not have support from the outside. But to make the journey worth the ride, we rode over many bumps along the way that only caused the enthusiasm to grow even deeper. The underdog fell in love with the vision of success for each other, and the rest is history!

The underdog, the Richmond High Oilers in our first season, was ranked as high as No. 3 in the state by the local newspaper polls. That was newsworthy on any day with any team, but for Richmond High, it was monumental news. This was the same team that *they* said could not do it.

The Oilers also showed a dramatic increase in their GPA through increased class attendance. I was not satisfied with average performance. I told my team, "Average is not good enough," I lived by that principle— and they began to live by it, too.

It became one of my mantras with them, to keep them focused on the value of effort and commitment: If you give one percent better a day, within a hundred days you're a hundred percent better.

Taking Account

Here is what accountability means to me:

Acknowledge
Consistent
Characteristic
Of
Unequal
Trust
And
Belief
In
Living
Integrity
Through
You

To get a clear understanding of this word, we have to realize that we are dealing with a compound word— one that is composed of more than one part. When we say "let's take into account" without understanding what the word "account" means, we fail to be productive.

Teammates, partners, coworkers, and family members are usually reminded that they are accountable to each other in many ways.

The dictionary defines "account" as "a narrative of records or events, a written or oral explanation of a business relationship involving the exchange of money or credit, worth or importance, and profit or advantage."

I referred to the dictionary because I believe that in order to get on top of things, we need to get below the surface of things. "Ability" is defined as "a form of power in any capacity, whether physical, mental, financial or social to perform a certain task or skill." When we combine "account" and "ability" to get "accountability," we can see the merger of both words, and the merging of the significance. "Accountability" then is in the sense of being able to put your activities in direct relationship to what is expected from that person within the defined boundaries of time, space, quantity, distance, etc. For example, you are responsible to take your test during the time you're given to take it or to finish the project by the deadline.

Accountability in itself is a form of responsibility, whereby a person takes on ownership to what is entrusted to him or her. It is absolutely impossible to be accountable when you fail to be responsible. There's an old saying, "If you fail to plan, then you plan to fail." When a student whines over his failing grades, but shows no plan of action for improvement, he or she shows a serious lack of responsibility. He or she is not accountable.

How can you effectively account for something or be accountable to someone when you ignore your responsibility? You might try to do so, but it is a lost cause. I've seen many situations where people who committed irresponsible actions attempted to give some form of a flimsy account which had no bearing. I speak from personal experience. When my basketball team at Richmond High failed to take their responsibility with their grades seriously, they then lacked the accountability to themselves, their teammates, their teachers, their parents, their communities, and to me, their coach.

It is imperative for us to understand the relationship between responsibility and accountability. They go together. Where you find one, you'll find the other. I take pride in myself as a successful basketball coach but to a greater extent as a mentor. Because of the latter, I naturally make references to basketball greats. Think of the Los Angeles Lakers of the seventies. Can you see Kareem Abdul Jabbar without Earvin "Magic" Johnson? How about Bill Russell without Earl "the Pearl" Monroe? The eighties to nineties era of the Utah Jazz with John Stockton and Karl Malone definitely spoke volumes. Although that duo did not celebrate a championship, they exemplified responsibility and accountability in their work with each other.

As the owner-operator of my sporting goods store in Richmond, California, I had a responsibility to my customers to make available to them quality products, delivered through excellent service. I had a responsibility to my employees to provide them with the necessary tools to get the job done to the customers' satisfaction. We strove to exceed the level of expectation in satisfaction. While I kept my end of my responsibility, I held my employees equally accountable for the distribution of the resources I supplied them with to get their work done. So as you can see, both go hand in hand.

A great story on accountability is found in the Bible, in Matthew 25. It tells of a business owner who entrusted thousands of dollars to three of his employees for investment. Two employees invested their monies while the third employee played it safe and hid his money.

It is quite evident in the story that those workers were all trusted with valuable assets (in other words, they were given responsibilities). The sad reality is that because one failed to take his responsibility seriously, he was unable to show accountability, in a profit-and-loss statement, when his manager returned.

Please do not subject yourself to such a poor level in achievement. Yes, we all have to start somewhere, but we should not be found at the starting point hours, days, months, years, or decades later, depending on the factors with which we're working.

As members of the Baby Boomers generation, we grew up with a one-channel black-and-white television with rabbit ear antennae and an old 45 RPM turntable. Someone took responsibility and changed things so today we have the electronic revolution of CDs, MP3s,

DVDs, plasma, and HDTVs. We must continue to move forward! In order to accomplish that, we must not only demonstrate, but live, walk, talk, and breathe accountability in every facet of our lives.

Help Is on the Way

There's a saying that goes, "No man is an island." In other words, you will have to work with someone else to get to where you are going. In order to do that, there must be trust and respect between people. When you have both of those values in you, you will build on being responsible, and then can be accountable to anyone. In this case, the outcome of accountability depends on responsibility that is founded on trust and respect.

You have to have respect for yourself, and let others see that, so they can then trust you to be responsible. Trust and respect are like identical twins with the last name of accountability. They look alike and act alike. This is a vital concept that I endeavor to graft into the minds of just about everyone with whom I come in contact. A scenario I hear of among some teens is their being upset that they're refused the key to someone else's vehicle.

If you had a car, would you trust the key to people you don't even respect? No, you wouldn't because you would not think that they are responsible, and for sure, they would not be accountable for your car. So if that's the case, you can see the need to build up the person's strong points, and keep building them one brick at a time. You can then build on the respect, then the trust, then the responsibility which will all lead to being accountable.

When I rode the kick scooter to Sacramento, I did it on behalf of the students, parents, and community of the Richmond High School system. It was taking responsibility with the conviction that something could be done, and that it would be done. I was not sure of how it would be done, but I followed through on my conviction. Someone needed to be accountable, to acknowledge that consistent characteristic. I was that person, with the trust and belief in living in integrity to make a difference for those students.

I am reminded of the young man who went to summer basketball camp with a group of kids from the inner city of the Fifth Ward section of Houston, Texas. This young man was the only one on the team who was not from that area. As a fifteen-year-old sophomore from a disciplined household, he told me he was very surprised at the "just get by" attitude of the team members. He took matters into his own hands by being responsible at every turn. He was at practice early. He stayed late. He hustled in drills and was enthusiastic about the game. He supported his teammates and obeyed the desires of the coach. When the summer was over, the volunteer coach expressed how surprised and impacted he was by the discipline the kid showed, so much so that the coach said he learned as he watched the young man show consistent responsibility and accountability.

In some cases, being like that fifteen-year-old is not easy. You must ask yourself some tough questions: Do you have any areas where you are lacking in your responsibility, and accountability? If we were to apply the principles of responsibility and accountability in your everyday activity, how would it add up?

Is there anything you would change when in front of others compared to how you perform in their absences? You know: "When the cat is away, the mouse will play"? Are you that way? Do you know of anyone in your circle of influence who acts that way? How about taking a stand in being responsible, and pass it on through your example.

I like to say that more is caught than can ever be taught. In your absence or presence to another person, you are a living example of responsibility and accountability whether or not you agree to it. You are being a role model, whether good or bad, so why not choose to be a good one?

I learned to be responsible from the "reality" of life with my family. My parents set a standard for their nine children; my seven sisters, my big brother Junior, and myself. I learned everything from watching my big brother Junior. He was the water and I was the sponge. I soaked up every ounce of water that he dripped into life's lessons. He modeled accountability before me and my friends by maintaining the high standards of the Carter family which my parents instilled in all of us.

You could say my family epitomized the hit television series of the sixties and seventies *The Waltons* with their beloved John Boy. I am a living example of my statement that more is caught than is taught. I caught it from my siblings. If you're in a situation without that family heritage, then start the family heritage by being a shining example of accomplishment through persistence and commitment. There's an avenue available for everyone one of us to learn and to teach responsibility and accountability. You should challenge yourself to be responsible and accountable, whether at home or at work. It is the way God intended us to be—and it is the effective way. Sometimes we overdramatize and tell ourselves that it is hard to do the right thing the right way. But as Nike says, "Just Do It."

Chapter Ten

Quality Role Models Never Hurt

Charles Barkley, the NBA Basketball Hall of Famer, once infamously proclaimed: "I am not a role model."

Whether you agree with him or not, he is a public figure whom millions of youths have admired. So his position on the subject may or may not be true. What is true, however, is that role models do matter, anyone can be a role model, and anyone can be influenced by a role model whether one considers himself role model material or not.

In one sense, Barkley was misguided. He claimed he was not attempting to be a role model, but he was one by default because kids were watching. If you know you are being observed and can be influential, to me you have a moral obligation to provide a positive view. Not just Barkley, but anyone.

His point was that you should not consider athletes

role models because you are not connected to them, that the role models should come from the home. As much as I agree with that position, too many homes in this country do not have positive role models for kids to emulate. Hence, they gravitate to those they see flourishing on television.

Of course, there is a real threat that comes with youths not having role models readily available, for the people they see on television or in their communities are not always upstanding individuals worthy of idolization.

Rather, the images—depending on where they look— are often people on the wrong side of the law. Movies and television still glamorize drug dealing and crime in a way that the youth in impoverished neighborhoods view as the only way out. To compound those warped images from the screens—featuring fancy cars, elaborate jewelry, and other over-the-top, illegally gained spoils— kids can look outside their door and see real-life bad influences that do not look so bad to a kid whose family is desperate for resources.

It Takes a Village

This is where teachers and school administrators come in. And mailmen, and Little League coaches, store owners—anyone who comes in contact with kids. It really is our civic duty to speak words of encouragement and advice or to be an example of success. It is important that we teach youths that success does not mean driving expensive cars and wearing ostentatious jewelry.

We have to impart in them that success should be measured in how someone masters his job, raises his family, helps others. That's the responsibility we all carry, no matter what Charles Barkley says.

Fortunately, I did not have to resort to the television for positive influence. I have lived my life under the influence of my role model and brother, Junior. What he did for me let me know I should be upstanding enough for my son and the young men I coached—and anyone I come in contact with. And that approach has allowed me to be effective in business, as a coach, as a man.

In short, I always was conscious that my actions could influence others.

Brotherly Love

I mentioned my brother earlier but not in the context of how much he influenced my life. He's the reason I believe role models are so critical. If he were some jerk who did things the wrong way, I would not have turned out as I have. I'm sure of that.

But he was all I needed him to be and more. Along with my parents, he had the greatest impact on me and is most responsible for what I have accomplished.

We called him Junior. He was the third-oldest child born in the Carter household, and everything he did, I wanted to do. He was a giant to me. I looked up to him, figuratively and literally. I wanted to be just like him. And all of my family and my friends looked up to Junior, too.

He was a hero, my hero. He gave me love, his time, and his attention. My brother would hurry home from school daily and complete his chores quickly in order to play with me. Mother would tell me that I had an internal clock that would let me know when it was almost time for my brother to arrive home from school. And I did. I would look up the road for him to come home from school at the same time every day.

He taught me so much. I enjoyed the time my brother spent with me. We had a close bond even though our ages separated us. My brother was ten years older than me, but that still did not stop Junior from teaching me everything that he knew about football, which was his best sport. When I was around five, I became his prized pupil.

He would get me outside and show me techniques. He would throw the ball to me, tackle me (but not hurt me)...nothing was off limits. His goal was to show me how football is played through playing with me and to toughen me up. So while he was much bigger, he used his size to throw me around to simulate what football felt like, but he was always conscious not to be too aggressive and injure me. He was remarkable that way because teenagers are quick to dismiss little brothers to chase girls or just do what teenagers do with their peers. I could not blame Junior if he wanted to do things that other teenagers did—shoot, that's what most of his friends did. But he made sure he spent time with me. He honored being my big brother, and as much as I appreciated it then, I appreciated even more as I got older.

The Star of Stars

While at Eva Garden High School, Junior literally stayed on the field the entire game, as he played offense, defense, and special teams. He was an incredible football player, setting records on offense. He would become the all-time leading rusher for the Rattlers. As a defensive player, he led the team in tackles and interceptions.

I looked on in amazement. This person who was such a football star was not only my brother, but also my brother who loved me enough to spend quality time with me. Best of all, our parents, pastor, and everyone in our little closely knit community liked Junior because he was a good person. He was humble and friendly and respectful. He showed me by his actions how I should behave. I was inspired by how hard he worked to become a great athlete and how everyone embraced him because of his humility.

I could not mess up the great reputation he built. Upholding the family name depended on my following his lead. That's what a role model does: Builds good people.

I share this part about my childhood to make this point: Charles Barkley was wrong. Everyone is a role model, and it is incumbent upon you to provide that example for those who are watching you.

My brother has been and remains that one person in my life that I look up to and still want to be like. That's how influential he was to me.

I recognize many people have grown up without that one person who served as a lightning rod and still had the ability to be successful, which is great. But here's the thing: Even if you have not identified someone as a role model, you should comport yourself—in business and in life—in a fashion that someone watching you would use as an example of how to live his or her life.

I doubt my brother even knew I was watching him as I was; he was just being himself. Although we never had much in the way of money, I consider my childhood a blessed one because I had a big brother to look up to.

Assuming Responsibilities

I also had five of the best buddies in Mississippi as my friends. I would not have traded those five guys for anything in the world. They were all different, but they had the common trait of loyalty. They let me know there are always role models among us, in ourselves.

It is disheartening to hear excuses made for men who shun their responsibilities because their father was not around to help raise them. That is not only an excuse, but a weak, shameful one at that. The reality is that not having a father should have the opposite effect. It should be the spark that makes sure you do not follow the same path. Which leads me to the value of family unity, be it at home or creating it in the work environment.

Simply put, the family unit must be strong and able to withstand any outside force that may try to break it down. It also has to withstand the internal in-fighting that sometimes comes with people who know and love each other so much that they can cause friction.

The foundation of that strength has to be love, honesty, and commitment. If those elements hold true, any inevitable attack on the unity will be rebuffed.

When I did not correctly execute a technique my brother showed me, he told me. He valued speaking the truth, which was also about love.

Love represents an unconditional affection that does not waver under any circumstance. Your sister may disappoint you or even anger you, but at your core you love her, and that love helps you push pass any other fleeting feelings.

Honesty helps build respect because your word is counted as truth. There is no doubt that sometimes people do not want to hear the truth and that the truth hurts. But honesty brings clarity, and we all operate much better and with more purpose when we have truth as the source of activity.

Commitment means there is a real desire and driving force that is unshakable. It fends off any notion of deviating.

The attempts to break that connection will come from many places, including peer pressure, which is an outside force that can act on one or more of the family members to alter family status. Whether it be thoughts, emotions, feelings, or actions, the outside pressure exerted on the family or the individual family member can be damaging. One family member can be affected and, in turn, affect the whole family unit in a negative way.

Some of the pressures or outside forces that affect family units today did not affect me while I was growing up. Today, our youths are introduced to things like drugs, sex, gangs, and alcohol much earlier and more prevalently. I am not saying that these things did not exist when I was growing up; I am saying that my family unit was so strong that these outside influences that were impacting others did not bother me. I had my parents, a big brother, and six older sisters that I could go to for help, guidance, and direction at all times.

Role models.

It was my siblings' responsibility to raise and care for me when my parents were not there. We all stuck together. We were a team. No one wanted to mess with us, because everyone knew that if you messed with one Carter, you had to deal with all nine of us. It was just a given.

Role Models Come in Both Genders

I had to think long and hard to come up with a phenomenal woman that I could compare to my top female role model, my mother. The only person I could come up with was the fairest African Queen that ever lived, but that still would not give her the justice she is due as my mom and an image for me to hold on to.

She reminds me a lot of the late Coretta Scott King, wife of civil rights icon Dr. Martin Luther King, Jr. She resembles the late Mrs. King's physical beauty as well as lifestyle. My mother stood by my father and took care in raising the Carter children while he was out providing for the family. Education was also important to my mom and the late Mrs. King, who believed in literacy for all children and loved each one of her children dearly. Mrs. King was a leader in her own right. She continued in her husband's footsteps after he was gone.

The story of how Mrs. King met Reverend King is similar to the story of how my dad met my mother as well. Mrs. King was hesitant to give Martin Luther King, Jr., the time of day when he first approached her. She let her guard down and agreed to speak with him. The rest, as they say, is history.

Finally, I look at the accomplishments these two women have made in their lives. They both had children and raised them during segregated and trying times for African-Americans. They kept their heads up and pressed on, instilling character and responsibility in their children. As I mentioned, I made my mother a promise while I was only seven. I promised her that one day a movie would be made about my life.

My mother believed in me more than I believed in myself. It is that belief and faith my mother has shown me over the years that keeps me striving and reaching toward new heights. She has been more than an inspiration and encourager in my life. She has been a driving force not only in my life, but also in my siblings' and her grandchildren's lives. Even though we lost our father some time ago, my mother has continued to press on and be instrumental in each one of our lives.

Her leadership passed down to my sister Ann, who as the oldest child, was a role model for all of us, a natural leader. It was through her venturing off from Mississippi to California that led to the entire family eventually migrating to Richmond.

She is not just an ordinary woman; she is a phenomenal sister, who showed me how to be a good, responsible brother. It was almost impossible for me to look at her and not see a wonderful example of how to be all those things.

Ann also resembles our mother, physically and internally. Her warm smile and sincere eyes could brighten a patient's worst day. She has always been a loving, caring, nurturing, affectionate, and unselfish person.

She was the Harriet Tubman of the Carter clan, in that she had an undying desire to lead and carry the burden of the family.

Harriet Tubman made nineteen trips to the South to rescue at least three hundred slaves. She made up her mind to escape from slavery when she learned that she would be sold again. Escaping to Philly, she saved up her money to return back for her sister, two children, and other family members.

Tubman was a planner. She made her escapes on Saturday nights knowing that slave owners would not have signs printed and posted for runaway slaves until Monday. She later would have a $40,000 price on her head. She carried a gun and was seen as armed and dangerous. She was there for a job and she was on her mission. It was only fitting that she was given the title "The Moses of Her People." Tubman saved many people in her lifetime. Her tombstone reads, SERVANT OF GOD, WELL DONE.

On a much smaller scale within our family, my sister Ann was like Harriet Tubman. She was a big planner and a risk-taker. She planned the trip for our family out West. She was a mother to her siblings. I look back over my life now and can only wonder where my life or the Carter family would have ended up if it were not for my sister Ann's love, leadership, and courageous efforts.

She is a role model because she was such an audacious leader. When it was time for me to make bold decisions in my life—including the many I made as coach of Richmond High, like locking out the team—I called on Ann's daring spirit to step outside the box to make a point.

Toughness Started at Home

My sister Stine was my role model for toughness. I gave her the nickname "The Enforcer." The moniker was so fitting as she had a tough personality. I learned through her that toughness was needed at times in addition to loyalty.

Growing up, Stine let her fists do the talking for her. I recall this fight on the school bus when I was about six years old. My sister Cookie had started a fight with another girl over one thing or another. The girl did not know that when you started a fight with one Carter, you definitely had to contend with more than just that person.

Even though Cookie had started the fight, The Enforcer was intent on ending it. I don't quite remember how it happened, but I can remember Stine just after the fight. She landed three girls on their backs on the same bus seat. I do remember seeing Stine's fist going across the three girls' faces in one smooth stroke. Needless to say, the three girls did not get back up from the bus seat. They did not want any more of what my sister had to offer. No one messed with Stine. They knew better. She is one woman I never want to cross.

That story is not to condone fighting. Rather, it is to make the point that she was my role model for being tough and for being loyal to family. She protected us at all costs. She had our backs, and her manner stayed with me—and I instilled what I saw in her with my team to be supportive of each other.

I also called on her fight when I did "Scooting for Schools." In essence, I was fighting for improved conditions at Richmond schools. It was something Stine would have done.

My sister Cookie got the name because she's "one tough cookie." But the other side of her was that she was quite emotional and could cry over things happy and sad. Her free showing of emotion showed me that it was all right to cry, to show you cared or that you were especially happy for someone. So, many times, when we had moving moments or achievements with the basketball team, I let the tears flow. If Cookie could do so and remain tough, I certainly could.

It was not a sign of weakness. It was a sign of strength that I could show my emotions without fear of anyone's perception—and it showed I had a heart, like her.

Strangers—What Are They?

My sister Hattie Jean was a role model for friendliness. She had an engaging spirit that I just had to emulate. If she met you, you were her friend—until you proved otherwise. That was her nature. And it is now mine.

I am a people person, which has helped me greatly in business. I often smile when I remind myself of Hattie Jean, who also had the most giving spirit, a sort of Mother Teresa.

Strangers were friends with her, and she would care for a stray wounded animal. When I spent money on my players for food or clothes or trips, it was with the spirit of Hattie Jean. She embedded in me the gift of giving.

My sister Grace is a gift, a role model of perseverance and inner strength. She has battled epilepsy all her life and yet you would not know it based on the way she picks herself up and keeps moving.

In my time at Richmond High, especially early when we were knocked down regularly, all I had to do was think of Grace to move pass the drama. If she could handle the physical trauma that came with the seizures she got, how could I not endure the trials I faced in trying to build young men into well-rounded people?

At times, those challenges I faced were so frustrating that I needed a level of serenity to compose myself. I wasn't always sure where it came from, but I know now: my sister Linda, a role model of control.

She is the epitome of peace and tranquility, someone who would mediate a volatile situation so convincingly that all sides had to listen and back down.

I know it was her spirit over me when I had to hold back my emotions as parents and administration called me every name they could think of when I locked the team out of the gym because of substandard grades. I saw how she many times held her composure in the face of duress, even as a kid.

My other siblings would fight, but not if Grace was there. She would negotiate a standoff as if she were a federal mediator. It was amazing. And I took that from her.

I took from my younger sister Debra her true business acumen. She was all about business, in her demeanor and actions. She took command of a room when she entered it. And she handles every situation professionally and with order. That's who she is and that mind-set rubbed off on me quite a bit.

So while Charles Barkley might have missed the point about being a role model, I do believe you can look around you, to the people close to you, and find traits in them that are admirable and that can help shape who you are. My family did that for me, and I know all that I am is because I had a house full of role models to emulate.

Chapter Eleven

The Coach Carter Impact Academy

We were on a multicity tour to promote the movie *Coach Carter* in 2005, and I was weary. I had no idea that pushing a film required so much of your time and such extensive travel. In the middle of the tour, in Dallas, we had some downtime and I decided to take a drive to no place in particular, but away from all the attention.

I went west on Interstate 10 and then east on Highway 6, with no final destination in mind. Finally, after about an hour, I exited at a small Texas town called Marlin. I had never heard of it, and at first glance there was nothing particularly distinguishing about it.

Then I drove around and I noticed so much that shocked and inspired me at the same time. I felt like I was in a time capsule from the 1940s or 1950s. The town had an eerie pre–Civil Rights Movement feel to it. Blacks mostly lived on one side of the main street called Live

199

Oak, where houses were not far from shacks. On the other side of Live Oak, whites lived in comfortable and, in some cases, palatial dwellings.

Even though they had taken down the WHITES ONLY signs, it was almost as if they still lived by that wicked, bygone code. My initial instinct was to get out of there, to someplace more in touch with today.

But another instinct came forward. About six years earlier, after I had done the 72-mile trek on a scooter from Richmond to Sacramento in "Scooting for Schools"—a movement to bring attention to the terrible condition of schools in our community—I formed the idea in my head to create a school that would counter all the ills I experienced at Richmond High.

Marlin, Texas, was that place.

Yes, it was a town I had absolutely no connection to or association with—unless you call understanding its need for someone who cares a connection or an association. Something just came over me as I absorbed the dynamics of the place. I felt it: The Coach Carter Impact Academy needed to be in that town just south of Waco.

Of course, there are countless places in America where upgraded schools are needed—every town in America needs them, in fact. I chose Marlin because in that moment I was moved.

There's a difference between being broke and being poor. Being broke is an economic condition, but being poor is a disabling frame of mind and a depressed condition of the human spirit. In Marlin, Texas, the people are both broke and poor. There is little opportunity for growth—and plenty of need for opportunities.

The Location

There are no industries in this town of 6,628 in Falls County. Sadly, it boasts the correctional system as its largest employer. There are three such facilities. There's the Hobby Unit, which houses female inmates in 1,342 beds. There's the Marlin Unit, which houses male inmates, in 606 beds.

When you do the math, that's a staggering number of citizens behind bars—1,948 out of 6,628, nearly one-third of the residents. So mind-boggling were those numbers that I could not believe it at first. But they were accurate, meaning something was seriously wrong.

In short, the young people in Marlin needed help, especially the young black people. With what we accomplished at Richmond High, I felt a civic responsibility to help where I could. Sadly, those in positions of authority in Marlin had no interest in helping kids. Moreover, they showed no interest in working with me. Instead of embracing the idea of a school designed to build leaders out of its young citizens, the powers that be in the city worked against me.

Marlin is an old town, with old money and people who are quite content with the sinful status quo. My house is located on Capps and Walker Street, which, back in the day, was off limits to blacks, except if they entered through the back doors of hotels, restaurants, or other businesses. Blacks just were not welcomed there and being caught on that side of town could have resulted in violence against them. But my overwhelming commitment to education added fuel to the town's unwelcoming stance toward my presence. My journey began there six years ago and remained steadfast to my mission.

Why? How? Because the young people need a fair chance at something better. Through all the virtues my role models instilled in me and my own dogged determination and stubbornness, I pressed on. The city of Marlin is just a microcosmic of what's happening in countless other cities across the nation. Marlin is suffering today from the same symptoms I experienced back in the 1960s in Richmond, California. And yet Marlin's plague comes in many forms:

- One of the highest teenage pregnancy rates in Texas.
- High rate of HIV of ages sixteen to twenty-five.
- Unemployment rate of more than 9.6% (compared to the nation's 9.1%).
- High crime and school dropout rate.
- Schools with standards so low the state is threatening to take over.

With that kind of rap sheet, you would think the city would be glad someone would desire to improve conditions. Instead, I found opposition, from townspeople and politicians and administrators. I learned at Richmond High and it was reinforced on this project that not everyone embraces ideas that I believe will advance youths.

Only thing missing from my detractors in Marlin were the bricks, water hoses, and attack dogs of the 1950s and 1960s in the South. The venom that was spewed was that sinister.

The Facility

I'm nothing if not a strong combination of determination and stubbornness. So the smirks from people and threatening letters and attitudes of disgust did not deter me. In fact, they actually fueled me to press forward. Who were they to stop me from doing something for our youths?

After deciding on Marlin, the next goal was to find a location. And sure enough, I identified a dilapidated building that had been abandoned for years. It was a former school on the side of town where blacks were hardly welcomed in the past. When you have a vision like I had, you can see beyond the unkempt grounds, the rooms filled with debris, the damaged ceilings, and the overall disrepair. In short, the building was a mess, but I could visualize a spit-and-polished facility that would become the pride of Marlin.

To get there would require so much. After acquiring the property and the land, I began a one-man cleanup campaign that took months to complete. But I got the building into presentable condition, which should have made people feel good about what was to come. Instead, even as my vision began to take shape with the massive cleanup, the opposition rose even higher. It seemed like there was a vengeance to get me to stop at all costs. I cannot explain why, except to deduce that many people there did not want to see anyone—especially an out-of-towner—shake the town's landscape.

Whatever the reason, the opposition executed several tactics to halt progress. There were false stories about me going to different divisions in the city to circumvent protocol. I was falsely accused of multiple citations by naysayers. There was even an incident where someone attempted to accuse me of having asbestos in the building. Unable to prove the accusation, someone actually placed asbestos material on the school property in an attempt to put a stop to the work in progress.

None of the attempted hindrances worked. I pressed forward by providing the proper documents and I was able to prove that the asbestos was planted and had it removed. That's how you have to work: with the understanding that your ideal plan might require some tweaking, which means you have to be flexible in getting accomplished what you desire.

The Mission

The nonminority families in Marlin do not support the school system. Their children are either homeschooled or they attend schools in the surrounding counties. From observing the people and their behavior toward my desire to bring about a positive change, I came to one solid conclusion about Marlin: The only time the town comes together is at a football game, where everyone is cheering for the same cause, the same outcome. During those ninety minutes or so, the social boundaries are dismissed and the townspeople come together in harmony. It is refreshing to see.

As soon as the game is over, however, they go back to their previous mind-set—you stay on that side of the tracks, and leave us on our side. Very sad.

The mission of the Coach Carter Impact Academy is to bring about a radical change by assisting in the growth of young people in personal development, academics, and athletics, resulting in improved socioeconomic conditions for them and their community.

My goal is to do just as the school is named, and that is to positively *impact* the lives of these students. I am dedicated to using my proven student-athlete model through programs directed to promote self-esteem and encourage excellence through focus on education, the family unit, and community service. I want to break the vicious cycle of child abuse through neglect in these young men's lives. I want to produce leaders for tomorrow, who will be productive members in society.

The first three years of the Impact Academy will be boys only. The idea is to start with males because, as a basketball coach, I have worked diligently with young men. We'd like to get off to a strong start in building our foundation and then, in Year 4—when we are running smoothly—we will integrate young ladies into our school.

The Academy is comprised of three entities. First, there's the school for academics and athletics; second, there is the Transitional Living Center, which will house sixty-four students; and third, there's the Emergency Shelter to assist in crisis situations.

I am a firm believer that general knowledge is no good until it is put in its proper place. My experience with getting the Academy transferred from an idea into a building confirmed my belief. Had I been more educated in the processes of opening a school, I would not have had to endure so much drama. I ended up learning a very costly lesson. There were numerous clauses and stipulations that I had to deal with. My lack of knowledge of all that was required led to the delay in progress. There were requirements for multiple building codes, city ordinances, state regulations, and general issues.

As a trustworthy person, I turned over the operations of the school to someone I believed was honorable. He wasn't, and it cost me thousands of dollars. I should have consulted with a specialist from the start, as every day there was a new challenge, sometimes built onto the unresolved challenges from the previous day. The depth of my desire to see the vision for the school to become a reality helped me stay the course despite these the daily challenges.

I held on to the notion that things would get better. But they got worse first. I had materials, tools, and monies stolen and time wasted. It was hard to fathom that people would be hell-bent on preventing a very worthy cause for our young people, but they tried.

The Coach Carter Impact Academy was birthed from my desire to offer more to the students in the form of education for life, to inspire young people through the much-needed avenue of education. The Academy is set to open January 4, 2012, highlighting a three-year journey that was not only difficult, but at times hard to believe. But I won. The opening of the school will be a significant day in my life and in the lives of the students and the city of Marlin. It has been a huge task just getting to this point. Hours of intense labor, as well as great physical, emotional, social, and financial efforts, went into the making of this upcoming celebration: the Grand Opening Ceremony of the Impact Academy.

A Unique Concept

We are taking a revolutionary, unconventional approach to education. The students are expected to excel in whatever task they undertake and will be held accountable. We will promote an environment of success that increases the students' sense of self-worth. By building confident, well-rounded youths, I believe we will produce students whose outlook on life will be one of hope and success instead of the oppression of today's culture there.

The Academy resides on ten acres of lush property;

COACH CARTER CARROT

Kids make up one-third of society, but they are one hundred percent of our future.

across the street from us are two mansions. We expect to accommodate up to 150 students. Our teacher-student ratio will be much smaller than the conventional school system to allow frequent and easy student-teacher interaction. Our classrooms are equipped with the necessary tools of today and state-of-the-art equipment to give our students every advantage to maximize their education. Every student will have a laptop. Classes will be conducted indoors and outdoors. Our children need to interact with the beauty of nature to gain an appreciation and respect for it. The students will experience much more than just a physical education class.

Additionally and importantly, the students will have structure in their lives. Organization is the foundation of success. They will be required to be on time for classes, meetings, and events, as well as other carefully thought-out directives that promote success. Other elements of the school include:

- **Study Hall:** The Academy is dedicated to providing professional academic tutoring in onsite classrooms. This is not optional.

- **Career Planning:** Assistance in enrollment in educational, vocational training programs.
- **Athletics:** The students will be encouraged to participate in daily athletic activities such as basketball, track and field, soccer, football, table tennis, strength and weight training, among others. Students will also be encouraged to participate in community team sports.
- **Small Business Operation:** There's a severe lack of knowledge of any business skills in the families of these students. The students will learn hands-on business management techniques by pairing up with an adult mentor.
- **Home and Gourmet Cooking Classes:** Students will learn and develop skills in meal preparation and menu planning. There will be a focus on nutrition. Students will have the opportunity to learn from the expertise of executive chefs in the culinary arts.
- **Life Skills Sessions:** Various workshops will be facilitated by qualified professionals. The students will be in groups of up to sixteen per class. Topics will vary, centering on relevant issues such as self-esteem, personal identity, decision making, communication skills, stress reduction, goal setting, and clarification of values. Emphasis will be on educating these young men on the appropriate management of feelings like anger, especially through despair. They will see sequences that

follow from when the underlying problem of anger is not tackled. They will learn to acquire and effectively apply the right mechanisms to recognize, control, and reduce anger, while able to maintain the dynamics of being assertive in a constructive manner.

- **Health Awareness and Prevention:** Workshops will be conducted by qualified professionals to target HIV/AIDS awareness and prevention. Other issues relating to a healthy lifestyle, such as dating, healthy sexuality, family planning, relationships, and friendships, will also be discussed.
- **Substance Abuse Awareness and Prevention:** Workshops will be facilitated by qualified professionals to address the problems caused by chemical dependency, drug and alcohol addiction—and how to avoid it.
- **Vegetation and Gardening:** The students will plant and produce their own supply of vegetables. They will become experts in their own way through planting seeds and watching the germination process take place. They will develop an appreciation for the farmers who labor to supply our grocers with fresh fruits and vegetables.

Clearly, we are doing things differently at the Coach Carter Impact Academy.

It is an approach that we believe will be the model of schools looking to impact students beyond academics.

Hours of Operation

The school will be in business from 6 a.m. to 6 p.m. I say "in business" because it will be run as a business and our business is education at every turn. Because most of these students have had substandard education, we will spend more time in the constructive environment just to catch up with other students. When the students leave school at 6 p.m., their class work, including "homework," will already be completed.

The success of the school is highly dependent on the unified commitment by all involved. Our ultimate goal is that our presence makes such a difference that the people of Marlin will see the value of the Academy and be compelled to get involved and support us, just to be at peace with themselves.

Already I am looking ahead to our first graduation. Our logo is a proud graduate in cap and gown, with diploma in hand, having blossomed because of the Academy experience. Our students will not just get by, because I firmly stand against "average." We will produce above-average students and people.

The second phase of our Academy is the Transitional Living Center. This center will house sixty-four students. We are fully equipped with sixteen furnished rooms, each accommodating four students between the ages of twelve and eighteen. The services in this center will focus on socialization, giving the students guidelines on how to live and function in today's society. The rooms are strategically organized, and the students are required to maintain clean and neat individual living spaces.

Students will have the pleasure of enjoying the sleeping arrangements and the comfort of being in their own bedrooms. From the beautiful curtains to the plush carpets, these rooms offer a sense of comfort. Still, a student in the Academy does not have to be a resident in the Transitional Living Center.

The residents of the Center are those students who, for whatever reason, lack total support at home, or those who want to attend the Academy but are unable to get there on a daily basis. Those students will be at the Transitional Living Center around the clock. There are many chores for the boarding student, including cleaning their areas, doing laundry, and cooking their own meals. These students will also learn the importance of being self-sufficient and productive individuals. They are expected to uphold the standards by adhering to a strict Code of Conduct. They are expected to set positive examples for one another, to, in effect, be one another's role models. They will accomplish this by being accountable in the classroom as well as in the residential hall.

The Transitional Living Center will have an on-premises staff to supervise the students. Graduates from the Academy can transfer into the Center and remain there in an active role through the age of twenty-one. This active role can be trade school or college preparation, but they will be productive in worthwhile causes.

The school has several homes in the area that serve as independent living quarters for these young men.

The third phase of the Coach Carter Academy is the Emergency Shelter. This shelter is a type of refuge for young people in crisis situations, which is prominent in Marlin. This type of shelter is not to be confused with the regular types of emergency shelters that are usually run by the cities or counties, and more often than not, poses serious threats to the needy person's safety. This shelter is a safe haven for a young person who might be a victim of some unpleasant event or for someone who is a runaway from home because of an abusive situation.

Words cannot truly convey the magnitude of this venture. I have had loads of help from many equally committed people, and I am indebted to them. Along with my faith and determination, they held me up during the many moments of trepidation over the three-year odyssey.

I will serve as chief executive officer and principal. I will be there every day to oversee the operations and work with the staff of teachers, who will be among the best around. I will interact with the students and be a beacon of what they can become.

For all that we accomplished at Richmond High, my expectation is to eclipse even that, to impact more kids. It is my experience as basketball coach at my alma mater that injected me with the spirit for impacting youths. And the Coach Carter Impact Academy plans to be an outlet that produces quality people who add something to society.

Chapter Twelve

Today's Real Athletic Achievements

Four years ago, long before LeBron James "took his talents" to Miami, I flew to Cleveland to participate in the NBA superstar's bike-a-thon for kids. It was so exciting and rewarding to see a global personality give so freely of his time to kids who admired him.

There were hundreds of people in attendance, and LeBron signed as many autographs as possible and touched as many hands as he could. He was as warm and engaging as someone could be.

I completed the five-mile ride—along with LeBron and fellow NBA stars Dwyane Wade and Tracy McGrady. Afterward, I watched in amazement as LeBron gave away brand-new bicycles to hundreds of youths. You could see excitement all over their faces; to get a new bike in the middle of summer—and from LeBron James, no less—was a moment those kids will never forget.

In fact, you can bet that many of them, for the first time in their lives, understood the spirit of giving and were motivated to do something as generous for others in the future.

I left there feeling like LeBron cared about his community. I saw the human side of the man, not the superhuman basketball player. There is nothing to say that you *must* do something magnanimous for anyone. The fact that he did that event—and so many others—tells me that he values his role as someone with stature and resources to help others and he identified with his community.

Wade and McGrady were equally committed and giving to the kids. They did not have to be there, especially during their off-season. But they were in support of LeBron and a wonderful cause. Each of them was gracious and made the kids feel comfortable in their presence.

James, like many professional athletes, has many causes he supports in an attempt to make things better for others. I was impressed that he teamed up with Duke University coach Mike Krzyzewski to support a program called "26 Seconds." It is a program designed to offset the alarming fact that every twenty-six seconds a child drops out of school. When we lose those kids, we're losing a part of our future.

To me, that is how you leave a legacy—whether you are a multimillionaire athlete or not. You do what you can for others.

A Rosy Future

Jalen Rose was a star as a basketball player at Michigan University and for a dozen years in the NBA. He grew up in Detroit and has always had an allegiance to his hometown. He showed just how committed he was when he teamed with city mayor Dave Bing to announce groundbreaking news on the Jalen Rose Leadership Academy, a college-prep high school with the goal of sending ninety-five percent of its students to college.

For someone like me who is a staunch advocate of education and someone who is opening my own school, I could only be filled with pride that Rose would take such a gigantic step to help children.

This is the same Rose who was a member of the "Fab Five" team in college that was controversial for its brashness on the court. He went on to play a dozen years in the NBA and became a standout analyst on ESPN. His comments in a documentary about his days at Michigan, when, as a teenager, he thought of Duke's African-American players as "Uncle Toms," set off a firestorm of controversy. Rose emphasized that those were his thoughts as an eighteen-year-old whose view was tainted and underdeveloped.

He clearly has matured over the years, turning into a man intent on developing and influencing young people. And just as he was in the apex of the storm, newspaper articles surfaced about his commitment to community. What he said in the *Wall Street Journal* sums up how he would like to be viewed: "I want to show [kids] that, not only do I care about them, but I am trying to do what I can to be a vessel to help them, unlock their future to put them in a position for success."

In Texas, where I live, David Robinson, the basketball Hall of Famer who played with the San Antonio Spurs, not only created the Carver Academy, a school in that city that focuses on high achievement, but also created the David Robinson Virtual Academy, which allows his impact on education of youths to span the country. His school is based on some wonderful principles: leadership, discipline, initiative, integrity, and service—great ideals. Robinson and Rose are two examples of good people doing something great, with the education of youths as the emphasis.

Making a Mark in Many Communities

As owner of the Dallas Mavericks NBA team, Mark Cuban has been known for collecting fines for criticizing referees as much as he is for turning around that franchise. Hardly anyone talks about the millions of dollars Mark donates in the name of helping others.

How about this? Every time he is fined, Cuban matches it and makes a donation to a worthy cause. Every time. When he was levied with the largest fine in NBA history—$500,000—he did not blink in matching it. He sent $375,000 to cancer research and $175,000 to Myofascia Pain Syndrome, a painful condition that affects the muscle tissue in one's face.

Not only that, but in 2003 Cuban created the Fallen Patriot Fund, which was established to provide support to the spouses and children of United States military personnel who were killed or seriously injured in Operation Iraqi Freedom.

It is easy to be cynical and say, "Sure, Mark Cuban is a billionaire and has money to shuffle out." But again, he does not have to do all that he does. Clearly, he considers having resources a blessing that he can bless others with.

Many of us, of course, do not have the financial resources to make a major impact in the same way Cuban has. But we all have time and talent to offer—and that is invaluable.

Reggie Bush: Skilled off the Field, Too

Before he started making spectacular plays in the NFL, I honored Reggie Bush with the "Coach Carter Award" for Excellence in Athletics in 2005. He was outstanding as a football player, but I was always impressed with how he carried himself. He was articulate and he dressed like he was earmarked for success.

Giving him the award in my name was special because I got to spend some time with him. The first thing he said to me was, "Coach, can you fire up my little brother? He just doesn't have it."

He cared—about his younger brother and other youths. His work off the field is commendable. He donated $56,000 to Holy Rosary High School near New

Orleans, a special education school that would have closed without his contribution. Then there was the $86,000 he donated to install artificial turf at Tad Gormley Stadium, which hosts six games a week because New Orleans schools do not have their own fields.

Additionally, among other acts, Bush introduced 619 Cologne, named for his hometown San Diego area code, and he designated a percentage of the profits for Hurricane Katrina relief.

Yes, he might be small in height, but he is big in stature. You don't give as he has and not have a big heart. I read where he said doing for others was natural for him, that anyone in his position would be equally giving. Sounds good, but not necessarily so. In truth, there are hundreds of athletes or people with substantial means who do nothing—or very little—and believe they are not obligated to be charitable. In the end, doing for others is a choice, a choice made by those who understand the value of helping others.

He Contributes More Than "Beans"

Kobe Bean Bryant, like LeBron, is among the few athletes in the world who can go just by one name; that's how bright his star is. But, also like LeBron, Kobe grasps the concept of being more than a player.

His Vivo Foundation—started in 2002—promotes education, reaches out to students who seek financial aid, and helps families of the men and women serving overseas.

Although he went directly from high school to the NBA, Kobe is a big proponent of education. He has paid for dozens of minority students to travel to Italy to study abroad and learn about a different culture through experiencing it.

I also like something I read from Kobe when he said he would not accept when people told him that he would not make it as a pro player straight from high school because he wanted it so badly. So, instead of being disheartened by the statistics or the naysayers, he became even more motivated.

He turned that negative talk into motivational fuel to become one of the greatest players ever. And when he was wrongfully accused of rape in 2007—a charge that was later dropped—Kobe did not recede to the background, on or off the court. He was just as dynamic as an athlete and just as committed as someone who embraces the inspiring message of how you must dream big because it inspires you to put in the work to reach your goal.

Japan's Tragedy Touched Lots of Hearts

There was hardly anyone who was not impacted by the tsunami and earthquake that ravaged Japan in 2011. Even if you were not from there or knew anyone directly affected, it touched your heart.

Imagine how global baseball star Ichiro Suzuki of the Seattle Mariners, who hails from Japan, must have felt watching the devastation of his home country in news reports of the earthquake and tsunami. Without hesitation, Ichiro donated 100 million yen to the relief efforts, which equates to about $1.25 million. The almost-daily fluctuation of the exchange makes it hard to pin down the value, but you clearly get the point. He stepped up with financial resources, which were desperately needed.

Many other players from a variety of sports made contributions to the Red Cross or other efforts to help the people of Japan endure their long battle to rebuild their wrecked land and property.

It is comforting to know that people come together to help people after a tragedy. Through all our own daily concerns, the human spirit breaks through.

And it does not have to be just about giving money, although no one can minimize the value of having the resources to get things done. Still, evolving into a person who cares and helps others is all about *doing something*. And while today's athlete often gets criticized for one thing or another, these are just a small percentage of the examples of giving young athletes around the world.

At the same time, doing for others is hardly limited to those with considerable financial means. Indeed, it is incumbent upon everyone to be a giver and there are many options, like being a mentor, with Big Brothers, Big Sisters or some other program; coaching in recreation centers and the YMCA; joining nonprofit organizations that tackle a variety of areas; tutoring youths after school.

So while high-profile personalities have been more visible in their contributions, all contributions matter and make a difference—in those you help and in you.

12 More *Tips for Success in Life from Coach Carter's Playbook*

1. You Are in Control of Your Own Character

It comes down to this in most cases: Who you are will dictate what you achieve. You must have a character replete with traits that demand the best of your God-given gifts.

Understanding who you are and what you are capable of will help you accomplish your dreams. But it is not enough to want to do something; you must have a spirit of achievement. And that spirit manifests itself in pushing forward through whatever obstacles to reach the desired destination.

That's having a character of achievement. No matter what the goal, it will not be a smooth trek to fulfill it. That's just how it is. There are always obstacles. But if your character or makeup is that of getting it done, you will push forward nonetheless.

2. Always Feel Good About *You*!!!

How can you be productive if you do not believe you can produce? Simple as that. Viewing yourself in a positive light means you will have an energy and a confidence to go about your business with zest and zeal. When you feel good about yourself, you communicate your thoughts and plans and ideas better. You are inspired by what the day will offer. You know you have something productive to offer—and you get it done.

3. Learn to Love Education

Not only should you seek information and knowledge at every opportunity, but you should develop a love for learning. It is the best and quickest way to be successful, as intense passion for learning allows you to access information that will arm you with the necessary knowledge to achieve beyond even your own expectations. The most educated person who flaunts multiple advanced degrees cannot hit a ceiling on learning because there is no ceiling.

And if someone like me, who has dyslexia, is an information hound, then everyone should be.

When you understand the value of learning, you devour books and newspapers and television programming, which enhances your mind.

4. As Hard As It Is, You Must Discipline Yourself

Let's say a close friend is having a party at the same time there is a seminar that will provide valuable information that can help you land a promotion at work. You know the party will be fun and the seminar, while informative, not so much fun.

What do you do?

The person who is not serious about advancing his or her career would pass on the seminar and attend the party. He would not be disciplined enough to sacrifice a projected good time for something he considers important to his career.

Ultimately, self-discipline and sacrifice go hand-in-hand. You cannot have one without the other. It takes a sacrifice to put in the hard work or to pass on the "fun" activity for the betterment of the job. And it takes self-discipline to make the sacrifice. Without those two traits, it will be much more difficult to be productive.

5. Think Outside the Box to Thrive Inside It

I'm not sure everyone understands the power of the mind. And I don't mean power like if you stare at something hard or long enough you can make it move. No, I mean that your thoughts control your actions. So if you speak it with integrity and honesty, you will achieve it.

Period. A person's imagination is the sum of his or

her dreams. And dreams are the result of your imagination. So if you do not dream of attaining a goal, how can you reach it? You have to put it in the universe.

This is not to say that all you have to do is imagine something and it will happen. We all wish it were like that. What I am saying is that for your goals in life, you have to first imagine them coming to fruition and then put in the necessary work to make them reality. But it starts with seeing it come together first.

6. Don't Be Scared; Have Courage

When you have ambitions, most times it takes something beyond talent to make them happen. In fact, it *requires* gumption or courage to even set out to do something significant.

You must call on courage to make your ambitions reality. The easy route is to wish for something great to happen, almost as if someone will deliver it to you. For too many, it actually is hard for them to take a leap of faith or to execute a business plan because of the fear of failure. You can't think about failure. You must be courageous enough to go for what you want. Otherwise, it just will not happen.

7. Be the Energizer Bunny

If you ever watch a college basketball game, you will see coaches constantly clapping their hands. Even if the player makes an error or the referee blows a call, often the coach will respond by emphatically clapping his hands.

You know why? Because the college coach gets it. He understands that projecting enthusiasm is the way to get the most out of their players. If they were quiet and subdued, the players would take on that demeanor. And their performance likely would be less productive.

There is a passion that is required in every form of business. You might not want to open a boardroom meeting by profusely pounding your hands together. But you should project an energy that permeates the room, that says to your audience: "This person cares."

An enthusiastic approach shows just that, which is important because when you're doing business, you want to convey that you care. That is paramount to leading your team—or being a part of a team. If you care, your people will care. If you are not a manager or a director, showing your enthusiasm lets your superior know of your commitment and energy toward the job, which is exactly what they want to know.

8. Image Really Is Everything

I could see by the looks on the faces of my players when they first saw me that they knew I meant business. You know why? Because I walked into the gymnasium that first day of practice in a suit and tie. They tried to ridicule me or joke about it, but the reality was that they knew I was there to do a job. So the image I projected from the start set a tone among the players.

In other words, you must look the part to *be* the part. There is no way around it: If we project an image of success, others will see us as successful and treat us accordingly.

It does you no good to *not* look successful. It gains you respect. It improves your image. And it makes you feel successful.

9. Have a Plan A, Plan B, Plan C...

No plan is foolproof, meaning somewhere along the way your best-laid plans have to be switched. So it would serve you well if you proceed with a level of flexibility so you can achieve the mission or goal no matter what obstacles.

Sometimes it is not even obstacles that get in the way. Sometimes the plan you devised just does not work. That's when we must put ego aside and go to a strong Plan B—and C and D, if necessary.

10. Do the Right Thing and Help Others

No way around it: We are here to help each other. This is not a spiritual proclamation. It is a moral responsibility.

I believe it is incumbent upon us to give abundantly

and without condition; do it because it is the right thing to do, not expecting anything in return. The thing about it is that you will be rewarded for your giving in one form or another.

Warren Buffett, Donald Trump...take any of the marquee businessmen and you will find that they are major contributors to a number of worthy causes.

We all have the opportunity to give—to charities, foundations, coworkers, youths, peers. There are limitless opportunities to adhere to moral responsibility. And it will make you feel good, too.

11. Understand That You Serve a Higher Power

I do not wear my Christian beliefs or spirituality as a neon sign for all to see, but it is at the core of my being. The faith I have in knowing there is a higher power that has blessed me, honored me, protected me...keeps me going in a meaningful direction with my life.

One of the Bible verses I live by is Luke 11:9: "Ask and it will be given to you; seek and you will find; knock and the door will be opened."

That's faith. And in life and in business, it matters that you have faith to carry you through moments or situations that perplex you and make you question what you are doing. It happens.

I know where my blessings come from, and that faith keeps me grounded and well aware that I am entitled to success.

12. Integrity Will Hold You Up

What does one have if not his or her word? Integrity matters a great deal in life and in business. It is about doing what you said you would do. It is about being up front and honest. It is about doing things for the right reasons. In the end, it is a state of being, a perpetual spirit of righteousness.

When you operate from a position of integrity, you function with a clear conscience, which allows you to go about your business free of internal turmoil.

These steps, worked together, promote a life of achievement and honor and business practices that will maximize you and your company's success and growth. My life is living proof of it. In whatever you do, there has to be a plan, a strategy, a road map...that leads you on a path of success. Follow it. Walk with your head up and your eyes open, and watch the things you desire begin to develop for you.

Acknowledgments

To my father, the late A. J. Carter, Sr., thank you for instilling in me what it means to be a Carter man—you and Junior will continue to be my role models and heroes. I could not have asked for a better father to share my life with here on earth. And to my mother, Hettie Lee Carter, thank you for giving life, strength, encouragement, your love, and your support throughout my life. I also would like to thank my seven sisters and brother: Diane, Ernestine, Cookie, Hattie Jean, Grace, Linda, Debra, and Junior. Your love and guidance has directed me in life from birth till this present moment. I thank you. It is because of you that I am who I am today. I am forever grateful and indebted to you. I love each of you dearly.

Thanks to Maxwell Billieon and the Billieon Group. Special thanks to Curtis Bunn.

Last but not least, my son Damien and my grandson Damien, Jr. (DJ).

Finally I thank all the women and men who have made great contributions to our world and our society. I commend you and applaud your endeavors.

Index

Index

Index

Index

About the Author

Ken Carter is the former Richmond High (California) basketball coach whose inspiring life story was captured in the 2005 blockbuster motion picture, *Coach Carter*, starring Samuel L. Jackson. "Coach" generated national news when he placed academics over athletics, locking out his undefeated and No. 1–ranked team because not all players had met his classroom requirements. In his seven years as coach he had 100 percent graduation rate among his players.

A former high school basketball All-American, he went on to become a prominent motivational speaker. In January 2012, he launched the Coach Carter Impact Academy, a groundbreaking school in Marlin, Texas, which will focus on academics, athletics, and life skills. The Academy would also offer dorms on campus for over 64 of the 150 boys in grades 8–12 who are facing poverty situations.

**BUSINESS
PLUS**

Recognized as one of the world's most prestigious business imprints, Business Plus specializes in publishing books that are on the cutting edge. Like you, to be successful we always strive to be ahead of the curve.

Business Plus titles encompass a wide range of books and interests—including important business management works, state-of-the-art personal financial advice, noteworthy narrative accounts, the latest in sales and marketing advice, individualized career guidance, and autobiographies of the key business leaders of our time.

Our philosophy is that business is truly global in every way, and that today's business reader is looking for books that are both entertaining and educational. To find out more about what we're publishing, please check out the Business Plus blog at:

www.bizplusbooks.com